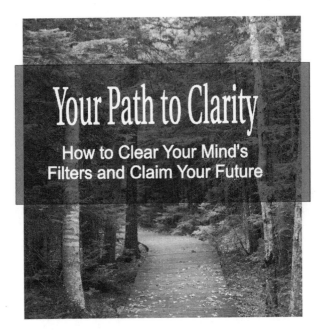

Your Path to Clarity

How to Clear Your Mind's Filters and Claim Your Future

Your Path to Clarity

How to Clear Your Mind's Filters and Claim Your Future

by

Jeff Londraville

LT Publishing
Longmeadow, MA

LT Publishing
Longmeadow, MA

Email: londraville8@gmail.com
Facebook: Jeff Londraville

Edited by: Valerie Utton
Cover by: Valerie Utton

Library of Congress: 2018902648

ISBN 13: 978-0-692-04702-6
ISBN 10: 0-69204702-6

Dedicated To:

My daughters Lola and Tyler
and
Everyone seeking clarity for their life

Acknowledgements:

My wife Christine, for always making me want to be a better man. I love you and love the way you love me.

Mom, Bob, Jill, David, Jimmer, and the rest of my family

My grandmother Mary Currier for always being there and making me feel that "everything is going to be alright"

My mentors, Kevin, Ted, and Roger – thanks for always being in my corner

My mentees, especially Andres

My editor, Valerie Utton

Contents

	Foreword	xi
	Introduction	xv
1.	How Did I Get Here?	1
2.	Whose Life is It? (Aka The Blame Chapter)	15
3.	Competition	27
4.	A Sense of Self	39
5.	Role Models	49
6.	Fear Doesn't Always Have to be Scary	65
7.	How Fear Impacts Our Choices	77
8.	Choices	87
9.	Experiences	101
10.	Self-Esteem – How Do You Like Me Now?	115
11.	Love	131
12.	The Plan	143
	Author's Bio	159

Foreword

I have so many memories....

Some not so great memories... one that was ingrained in me when I was thirteen years old as a permanent reminder of who I never want to be.

I remember opening the door to our small second-floor apartment and walking in to see our "rent to own" dining room table, in pieces on the kitchen floor, with my passed-out drunk father lying on top of the rubble. Glass from the table top was everywhere. My father had several small cuts on his face, neck, and arms. I remember the table base of gold and black aluminum pipes, now bent and flattened to the floor, surrounded by shattered glass, beer cans, and other illegal substances. I remember my brother picking our father up and helping him shower while I picked up the mess. I remember helping clean and bandage his cuts and bruises. I also remember turning him on his side in the middle of the night as he vomited into the well-placed waste basket and thinking that life would be so much easier if he weren't around.

On that same night, it was my turn to stay up with our clinically depressed mom. She'd been having suicidal thoughts and would disappear in the middle of the night for drives, so my brother and I took turns (with my grandmother when she was around) staying up in the living room with her to help her get through another tough night. She told her doctors she wanted to end it all by wrapping our twice-repossessed minivan around a tree. She made it through that night, but shortly thereafter, we checked her into a psychiatric facility so she could get the help she needed. At some point that night, I closed my eyes for an hour or so and then had to get ready for school.

The next morning during my lunch period I went to find a quiet spot. All I was looking for was a place to take a minute to cry, punch something, or just breathe. I walked into a room which I thought was empty, but it wasn't, and that moment changed my life.

I think we can agree that any individual going through these kinds of situations on a weekly basis would suffer from the effects of them right then, and possibly for years to come. But can you imagine what situations like these will do to a young person just about to enter high school—a time that brings its own complexities as we try to figure out who we are, how to fit in, where we fit in, who and what defines us, and who we want to be?

I think it's safe to say that at thirteen, a crucial age for all young adults, I was experiencing a low point in my life.

With that said, how does a young person going through experiences like the ones mentioned overcome them rather than succumb to them? Or understand how to break the cycle rather than repeat the cycle? Or to not be weighed down by these experiences versus being elevated by them?

For me, *Your Path to Clarity* is more than just a book. This is how I operate now. This is how my mind is trained to think, and how I live my daily life. And this has been my journey since the age of thirteen. What you don't know is that the ideas in this book became a part of my success story before a single word was ever put on paper.

When I walked into that room thinking it was empty, that was the first time I met the man who became my mentor, my father figure, my friend, and the author of this book, Jeff Londraville.

One thing I've realized over time is that as we mature, we develop an ability to look back at certain moments in our life and recognize them for the crossroads they were. Walking into that room and having the first of many, many conversations with Jeff was the first crossroad in my life.

That morning, I didn't know if it was that my troubles were written on my face for the world to see, or if Jeff's years in the field of education working with students in urban environments led him to read my demeanor. Now I know it was because that's the kind of person he is... a person who just cared enough to look and sincerely ask one simple question, "How are you?"

It has always been uncharacteristic for me to share my personal life. Even writing this foreword was very difficult. I was raised by old-school parents (and sometimes grandparents) with the mentality that what happened inside the household was private and not to be shared. In their minds, seeking or asking for outside help was demonstrating weakness. But for whatever reason, that day I didn't care. I didn't think, I just vented. He listened. He didn't give advice. He just listened.

As I walked out of that room I remember him telling me, "Roll your shoulders back and keep your head up." I remember thinking *how cliché*. However, he didn't mean this in that stereotypical manner. I found out in another conversation that there were two reasons he was encouraging me to make this simple change. It wasn't just that he didn't want me looking defeated as I walked the school halls, but he also believed that the first step to making a change was taking a first step.

The next day he looked for me and asked how I was doing, and from that day forward Jeff and I had open and honest conversations about life, our similar backgrounds, and most importantly, what he'd done to succeed and overcome the big obstacles in his life. I learned how he had not let his surroundings define who he was or who he was going to be, and how he was able—as I would be able—to take the negative memories and experiences and filter them to extract the positive lessons within.

We shared candidly. He gave advice and utilized several school programs to distract me and hone some of the talents he saw in me. There were times when we disagreed, and times when I didn't listen to him—most of which I ended up regretting. But there has never been a time when I doubted his honesty, or a time when I didn't believe he had my best interest in mind. And now, after 18 years of friendship, I can honestly say, without hesitation, I am a better man, better friend, and better son because of the advice he's given me.

And now he's sharing this life changing advice with you. I encourage you to read it and take advantage of what's being offered so you can clear your path to clarity. It isn't impossible. You can get past the blocks that made it feel impossible. It has been put into practice by me, and it helped me change the path I was on.

I have so many memories....

Some not so great memories...but I have still developed a path of clarity towards a great life.

Sincerely,
Andres Gomez

Introduction

Why does it feel like life is so hard sometimes? Why is it that we can't seem to get out of our own way? We want to understand and figure out the answers to questions like these, but it's hard to do it on our own. And when we don't find answers, we're more likely to end up battling with life instead of working with it—or even enjoying it. We end up feeling anxious and depressed, or just plain old ordinary struggle with the past. I've had my struggles too, so I know how difficult it can be. That's why I wrote this book. I want you to be able to look at your life through a lens that's clear of the all clutter our minds tend to collect. Most of it wasn't ours to begin with anyway. It was contributed by other people, places, things, and events, and now it's time to get some clarity about what is, and isn't, worth keeping. This book will help you through that process so you can clearly see a path to being the person you want to be.

To get there, there is one reality that has to be accepted: The choices we have to make in life aren't always easy to make. Sometimes people take jobs they'd rather not take because it's the best solution for their family, or because they need the money. People stay in unfulfilling or painful relationships because they think it will be better for the kids, or simply because they're too afraid to be on their own. And sometimes in life, the best path isn't clear.

To make better choices, we have to ask ourselves questions that will get us to dig deeper. The danger of not asking questions is becoming trapped in situations that feel very far away from where we hoped and dreamed we'd be. When that happens, it seems like the easiest solution is to just give up on our future. But trust me, giving up on your hopes and dreams is never a good choice or path—not when there are so many possibilities to consider. And I know that's a scary thought too, the idea that you might have to make more choices when you're already feeling trapped or off-track with the choices you've made so far. That's one way this book is going to help you. It's going to help you uncover a serious majority of the junk that's been residing in the spaces between you, your choices, and your path.

Now, think of a camera. When you look through a camera's lens, you see a picture. In a very real way, this is also how most of us look at the world. We look at it through our own personal lens. However, two people can see the exact same thing and have completely different views of what they're seeing. For example, a teacher assigns a five-page paper. You see that paper as a path to raising your grade while a classmate sees it as a sure-fire path to failing the class. So while we all look at the world through a lens, we each have filters that we use to process the information we're taking in. Our filters develop in ways that are unique to us, which is why we are all so different.

A paragraph ago, I said this book could help you clear the path between you and your choices. Each chapter in this book focuses on one of the ways the people and experiences in your life might have influenced, shaped, cluttered, and/or clogged the filters you use to make choices and decisions. If you don't take charge of your choices and decisions, your filters will continue to be developed and shaped by the people and situations around you—for better or for worse—regardless of your wishes and dreams.

No one escapes this reality. We are all influenced by the people around us, especially in childhood. Some of us have had good role models, and some of us have had bad role models. But there's no doubt that the decisions we make in life about careers and partners and attitudes are affected by the people around us—both past and present. And sometimes, the information and feedback we get from all those people interferes with the filters our mind uses to interpret and understand our world.

Our filters can reveal how much we've been influenced by the people in our lives too. For example, if the people around you keep telling you that you aren't smart enough to become a doctor, then you might choose to avoid going to medical school even if it's your dream. That's an example of looking at life through a filter that's been shaped by outside influences. The result of those influences was a choice that's different from the choice residing in your heart.

As an author, mentor, teacher, and fomer school administrator, I understand the influences students face every day. I've seen how the choices they make during their transitions from childhood to adulthood are affected by the filters they look through, and by the fact that they're still struggling to understand who they really are and what they really want. Adolescence is not an easy time for any of us, but the process is even harder when we can't get to our own thoughts and concerns because we're dealing with all the thoughts, beliefs, concerns, and expectations other people have imposed upon us.

As a young man, I felt the influence of living in a violent home. My mother and father divorced when I was eight years old—and they needed to. Their relationship did not work. Unfortunately, my sister, brother, and I were dragged into the conflict. So I know how hard it is to define your identity amidst the struggles of life. But I also know how powerful it is to clearly see your path ahead of you, because I've done it. The result was finding a rewarding career, having a loving family, and developing the ability to help others.

I know you've been influenced by others because we've all been influenced by others. No one grows up in a vacuum. No one escapes the words and deeds of others. From the moment we're born, our minds are constantly trying to make sense of the information we're getting from the world around us. It would be great if we were all born with an instinct for distinguishing between helpful and harmful influences, but we aren't. It isn't like there's a class where we learn about our life either. Our filters start to develop, but they get blurred by other people's influences and then it's hard to figure out what's really going on. The result is a struggle to make clear unbiased choices and decisions that will save us from ending up in places we don't want to be in, with people we don't want to be with.

Life doesn't have to be like that. We can see life through a clear lens. We can clean and clear our filters and make choices and decisions that are better for us. But before we begin with how to do that, I'd like to address some common misconceptions about what it means to read a "self-help" book, or to follow a personal development program.

Too often, the word "help" is associated with weakness or incompetence. People fear asking for help because they think others will view them as weak or needy. Nothing could be further from the truth. Seeking help—be it from a book, a therapist, or a friend—is an act of courage. To admit that you can't do it all on your own is a sign of maturity and growth. Too many people avoid seeking personal improvement or growth simply because their filters have been so overly influenced by others that it's hard for them to believe they have a right to feel better about who they are, or where they are. Instead, they get caught up with making excuses and blaming their failures on everybody and everything else around them.

You aren't going to do that. With this book, you're stepping up and saying, "I want to take control of my life so I can move forward." And yes, taking responsibility for your life can be scary. But by taking control of your life, you'll also be in a better position to help others, and that's a powerful gift. So here are few concepts to consider while you're reading....

— *Learning*: Many people look at this word in a negative way because it's like admitting that they don't know something, and that means they're vulnerable. That kind of interpretation is reflective of one of the negative thought processes this book will help you filter out. "Learning" means you are seeking to know more, which means you're looking to improve some aspect of your life.

— *Counseling*: This means putting learning and helping together. There are many aspects to counseling. We can follow our own "inner" counsel by reading books, researching our problems, and listening to people who motivate and/or inspire us. We can take it a step further and seek one person's counsel through individual counseling. We could pursue group therapy. Following this path doesn't mean we're crazy, or too helpless to help ourselves. It's a course of empowerment and choice. The value of seeking counsel from a qualified person is that you'll always know there's another person who has your best interest at heart.

— *Choice*: Above all, this book is about choice, and acknowledging the truth that only you can make the choice to take control of your life and set a plan for who you want to be, and where you want to go. This book can help you clear your filters so you can look though your lens and see the world as it really is, but if you don't embrace the active and ongoing process of choice, you're filters—and ultimately your path—will slowly and surely once again become clogged.

Learning about filters can be an exciting process. There's something very empowering about realizing that you might not have had a clear picture of what was going on before now. Claiming ownership of your filters is the first step in claiming ownership of your life. That doesn't mean you aren't going to make mistakes, or that all your choices will always be easy—life rarely works out that way. But you will realize that if your choices can get you into a situation, there's probably a way for your choices to get you out of it, and that sometimes, the most difficult choices can be the most rewarding. The way to increase the odds in your favor is to clean your filters so that you can clearly see through your lens to the world beyond. This is a choice that is completely within your power to make.

Jeff

No one saves us but ourselves
No one can and no one may
We ourselves must walk the path

– Buddha

1

How Did I Get Here?

We come into this world with a fairly clean slate. We're born without a set career path, educational agendas, or habits other than those we perform by instinct. We don't know who we're going to be when we grow up, or what we're supposed to do.

As we grow, our thoughts and ideas about what we want to be like, what we want to do, and who we want to our spend time with start to take shape. We watch the world and start imitating what the people around us do. As we get older, we start making decisions about the behaviors we see.

We watch the behaviors our parents model for us. If we like them, we follow their example. If we don't like them, we vow to "never be like them." It would be great if our parents or guardians always modeled good behavior, but they're human, so they don't. The problem for us as young children is that we don't know the difference between inherently good or bad behaviors. All we know is how it feels to be around those behaviors.

Once we start school, there are teachers and other adults trying to reinforce "appropriate" behaviors while discouraging behaviors they consider inappropriate or ill-advised. For the most part, those reinforcements are for the betterment of everyone. Being told not to hit people and to be polite is something that serves the greater good. Schools would be in chaos and society would be a mess if we didn't all agree on at least some basic rules of human behavior. But even when reinforcements are meant as a benefit to the individual as well as society, many reinforcements—even seemingly good ones—can impose limits on the way a child will think about themselves.

When Well-Intentioned People Get in the Way

Even a well-intentioned parent can harm a child's self-esteem by trying to direct their child away from a future of potential disappointments or failures: "You're so good at writing, why don't you try to work as an editor?" A guidance counselor might offer what they think is good advice: "You seem to struggle with science and math, so maybe becoming a doctor isn't the best choice for you."

Statements like those are usually intended to keep a child safe from future hurt or harm. The people saying them are very often well-meaning and even caring people, but they are speaking through their own filters, and in the end, their words can be stifling and limiting and just as likely to cause pain.

It takes time for children to grow and develop their ability to make decisions about the quality or validity of what people are telling them. That's why we remind our children not to speak to strangers. They don't have the ability to sort out and discard the negative outlooks, ideas, and beliefs being foisted on them by parents, care-givers, guardians, role models, and yes, strangers. A child can't see all the disappointments, failures, and hurt fogging the filters of the people they come in contact with. Again, a vast majority of those people are well-intentioned, but that doesn't change the fact that what they're really doing is imposing their own world views on someone who will look up to them and listen to what they have to say simply because that's what they've been taught to do.

It's not fair to expect a child to understand that everyone sees life through their own filters. There are adults who don't understand this idea; adults who never realized it would be okay if they thought differently, or chose to believe something other than what they learned when they were growing up.

Our childhood may lay the foundation for our personality, likes, and dislikes, but it is not the single defining source that determines who we become. Everybody's filters are influenced by the way they were raised. This isn't an attack on the way our parents raise us either. On the contrary, understanding that other people have filters influencing the way they see life will help us identify which behaviors exhibited by our parents or guardians we wish to embrace, and which ones we're ready to discard.

The goal is to view the world with a clarity that is based on who we are rather than on how we were raised. The course of our life does not have to be determined or decided by the disappointments and anger of the people who had the power to influence us. We grow up, and as we do, we begin the process of molding and defining our filters in ways that define us. Ultimately, our life is ours to define.

Understanding

For many of us, looking back at childhood is a painful exercise. Sometimes it feels easier to suppress our negative experiences, or to try and forget them altogether because the thought of examining what happened would be like reliving them all over again. Some people hold onto the negative experiences in their lives as if they are trophies of things that have happened to them. They say, "Look at my scars," and use them as justifications for not pursuing a fuller life. It may be scary to think about doing something, but giving in and wasting your life because of what other people have done to you is like declaring them the "winner."

It's understandable why someone might not be ready to give up the hatred they feel for their parents or guardians too. After years of hearing and experiencing the same things, they don't know how else to define themselves and their resentments become a part of who they are—it's all they know. The anger they might feel as a result can become a powerful motivator. It could give them purpose, but it could be expressed in other ways too: lashing out, withdrawing, promiscuity, and experimenting with drugs.

If any or all of these sound like you, please know that you're not alone. It's important to remember that no one is born with these behaviors. They are the result of the powerful influences you observed and absorbed as a trusting and impressionable child.

We all have our trophies and stories. They are proof that we have good reasons for not moving on. And sometimes, the pain we know is more comfortable to live with than the fear of the unknown life we could be living. Instead, we settle for carrying our burdens around in an emotional gunnysack, ready to pull them out so other people will understand why we are the way we are. It's a perfectly natural thing to do. But the past can be a heavy weight to bear. The longer we carry it around, the heavier it gets, and the more influence over us it has.

To move on from these experiences, we need a way to

make sense of what happened. The advantage you have is that you're learning about the different ways filters can influence the way we see and experience the world, and how other people's experiences can seriously influence the way our filters develop. The people who are responsible for our negative experiences probably still don't have a clue what a filter is. They don't know their filters have been compromised. They might be so oblivious that they don't not even realize their actions had an effect on us. They're still struggling with the difference between who they are and who they'd hoped to be. They're still interpreting the world through filters chuck full of the perceptions and biases drummed into them by their parents, guardians, role models, and society.

But they are people, just like you or I, and even though their actions may have been negative, we're the ones who get to decide the impact their actions will have on us from this point forward. Making sense of what happened doesn't mean dismissing their actions or forgetting what they put us through. This is more about grabbing hold of the truth that everyone's worldview is unique to the person experiencing it.

Everybody has their reasons for doing things. When we take the time to try and put ourselves in someone else's shoes—even if it's just for a minute—we might find some context for what they've gone through. Being able to do this is a huge advantage for us. For one thing, as we move through our life and deal with new people and new situations, we'll be better prepared to deal with the things other people do.

One example of how this might play out in real life is with abandonment. It's normal for children to grow up believing their parents will always love them, take care of them, and be there for them. But what happens when a child is abandoned by a parent? How is a child supposed to make sense of that?

Children aren't equipped to deal with a situation like that. Without knowing what to do or how to fix it, they're likely to develop insecurities over a situation they had no control over. They start feeling as though they weren't good enough. If they had been, the parent wouldn't have left. Or they might decide they must have done something wrong to make their parent walk out of their lives. They think that if they could just get it right, everything would be okay. As they continue to grow, they might start blaming the missing parent for not being there and using that as an excuse for antisocial behavior. "Well, I don't have a dad, so that's why I act this way," or "Nobody cares about me anyway, so why should I care about anybody else?"

Having a parent leave the home without notice or communication can be a horrific experience for the entire family, but children tend to suffer more because they don't have the coping skills to make sense of what happened. Instead, they feel overwhelming sadness, a sense of loss, resentment, anger, and frustration—all natural responses to struggling with the idea that their parent doesn't want to be with them anymore.

So now the question is, how does someone move on from a situation like that? Maybe the first thing to do is to accept the fact that as children, we have very little control over what happens in our lives. We don't get to make the decisions about where we live, or about who our parents bring into the home. If we did, then we'd have a whole list of reasons for why we should live somewhere, why someone shouldn't be able to move into our house, or why our parents should stay together and work their problems out.

It's the same for parents. They have a whole list of reasons for making the decisions they made too. And their list of reasons will always be different from our list because parents see the world from an adult perspective. Sadly, they often get so caught up in their own drama that they don't always do a good job of explaining what's going on. We can ask and hope for clarification, but even when they make an effort to explain, it can be hard to understand or accept their reasons.

The challenge in this situation is viewing the parent's mindset at the time of the abandonment. At some point, we all develop the ability to understand that people make decisions based on what's going on in their own heads. They make those decisions through the filters in their mind. When their filters are blurred, they're less likely to make good decisions for good reasons. The more blurred a filter is, the more likely their reasons are to be the result of what they experienced and learned when they were growing up. We can't wipe their filters clean though. More importantly, *it's not our job to unclog, unfog, clean, or clear someone else's filter.*

This isn't about deciding to feel sorry for them either. It's about taking a step back and viewing our childhood from the perspective of the people who were around us. What happened to them? What might have motivated a parent to leave? It may have been due to selfishness, fear, or drug abuse, but this isn't about finding a reason to blame them or forgive them. It's about understanding that the person who left was struggling.

Whatever the reasons end up being, each one holds the absolute truth—that the parent did what they did because they were overwhelmed by the reasons they had in their own head. One of those reasons may have been because they really thought it would be better for their children in the long run. Or they may have truly believed that leaving was their only option. They might have been wrong, but they're human beings making choices based on filters that have never been addressed.

Once we start searching for, and recognizing the perspectives and motivations of other people, we begin to realize how much of our life has been influenced by the people around us. But examining our past and analyzing the path we've been set on doesn't mean focusing solely on the negative. Nor does it only apply to people who've had traumatic backgrounds. Everyone is shaped by their childhoods. Clearing our filters isn't just about getting rid of the bad stuff, it's also about being able to identify and embrace the parts of our childhood we want to hold on to while we're looking for our own direction.

The Teen Dilemma

Teenagers are often caught between childhood and adulthood. They don't have the life experience necessary to make major decisions about career paths and higher education, which is why their parents, role models, and guidance counselors try to help them make those decisions.

Teens don't always have a sense of their own power either, or the confidence to speak up and ask questions. But that won't stop people from telling them it's ultimately "their" decision to make—right after they tell them what they "should" do. In the end though, it's the teenager who will carry the weight of the consequences of their decisions and actions, even when those decisions and actions were influenced, or straight-up made by those well-intentioned people.

It's a dilemma that leaves many teens confused and unsure of which way to go. Their decisions are made all the more difficult by their natural desire to please (or in some cases to rebel against) the influential adults in their lives.

If you're a teen or even a young adult and you're in that position, there are questions you can ask yourself when you're starting to make plans for your future. It's true that you may not have had a lot of "worldly" experiences, but you can still evaluate your life up to this point.

- What's been working for you so far?
- What hasn't been working?
- Where have you been?
- What do you like about where you live?
- What do you like to do? What do you hate to do?
- What have you liked and disliked about your life so far?
- What about the people around you? Who do you like and dislike?
- Do you see your parents as people you would like to emulate?
- Are your mentors living lives that seem commendable to you?

That may seem like a lot of questions to answer, but you'd learn a lot. Answering questions like these will help you realize what works and what doesn't work for you, and help you make better decisions about how you would like to shape your life. They are good thoughts that can help you start designing the life you want to live.

Other people might have already asked you some of those questions. If that's the case, then you already know that there are some people who ask questions as if there is only one correct answer. They know the answer, and they expect you to get it right on the first try. They might be asking those questions for all the right reasons, but it's okay to remember that the answer they have in their mind is going through at least one of their filters, so you might have an answer that's different than theirs.

Don't put off asking yourself these questions though, or be too afraid to ask them either. It's true that you may not be used to taking on this kind of responsibility. It's true that it's easier to put off making decisions too—especially when your deadlines are far away. But the longer you put them off, the more likely it will be that you will have to surrender your decision making power to people who believe they can make better decisions about what's best for you.

When I ask teens what their thoughts about college are, they often respond with questions like, "What college should I pick?" If I ask them what they want from a college, they don't know how to answer because they haven't thought about it. They didn't know it was a question they could have asked themselves. Even adults have problems with slowing down long enough to ask the kinds of questions that will help them take control of their lives.

If you asked most adults, "What makes you comfortable in life?" you'd likely get a blank stare back. Too many adults have conceded comfort and happiness for what they think is needed to secure a good career and support their families. They can't even remember what they wanted for themselves when they were teenagers.

It's never too early—or too late—to start considering your filters. The reason your filters are so important is because they will help you understand what makes you feel the best. They will help you decide if opportunities that come along are compatible with what you really want to see in your life.

You may not know this yet, but you're your own best teacher. You already have a past full of reactions to experiences you can look back on to help you consider how you might react to something in the future. We all instinctively know what feels okay, but when our filters get blurred or fogged over, we end up doubting and second guessing ourselves and our intuition. Sadly, too many people ignore their intuition and end up with laments like, "I don't want to be this person" or "I hate my job" or "How did this happen?" Too many people let life happen *to* them without realizing they have the power to clear their filters and improve the quality of their choices, their decision making, and ultimately their lives.

Flexing Your Filters:

Now that you're beginning to think about your life and where you are right now, it's time to start thinking about what you want for yourself—as opposed to what other people want for you.

Make a list of five things you dream of being, doing, or having in your future.

1. _____

_____

_____

2. _____

_____

_____

3. _____

_____

_____

4. _____

_____

_____

5. _____

_____

_____

Now, look at each item on your list and write down where the original idea came from. Most things we dream of being, doing, and having don't pop into our minds out of nowhere. I'm not saying that your dreams aren't your own. They are, and you've made them your own. What I am suggesting is that it can be very interesting to investigate the source of our inspirations.

1. _____

_____

2. _____

_____

3. _____

_____

4. _____

_____

5. _____

_____

2

Whose Life is It?
(Aka The Blame Chapter)

It's an easy to question to answer. It's your life! And just like everyone else's life, yours is shaped by your childhood. Now that you're learning how filters help you define what you see when you look around, there might be a tendency to zero in on the negative filters, forgetting the good filters you've developed too.

Anyone who has ever fallen in love knows what it's like to look through a love filter. It almost doesn't matter what happens when you're looking at the world though a love filter—you love everybody and everything. We can also develop filters that help us recognize opportunities for generosity, kindness, acceptance, and many more positive attributes.

The process of looking at our filters isn't just important for people who've had traumatic backgrounds either. Taking control of your filters isn't just about getting rid of the bad stuff. It's also about being able to identify and embrace the parts of you that you want to hold on to while you're finding your own direction.

Every parent and guardian knows that at some point in time you'll be taking control of your life. So far, a majority of your life has been decided for you by people helping you or guiding you in directions they think are right for you. Making the decision to take control is both exciting and challenging.

Even if you were raised by loving parents who supported your hobbies and passions, you're still likely to have questions about whether or not you want to follow in their exact footsteps. You may decide you want to be as compassionate and supportive as they were; but you might also realize that the positive reinforcement they provided steered you towards certain activities while putting limits on others. Here's an example...

John is an A student with loving parents. His father recognizes that John is good at math and drawing, so he encourages John to be an architect. He helps John look for colleges with good architectural programs and buys John books about design. John decides to pursue a career in architecture, but he isn't really sure if it's because his father believes he would be good at it or because he has a genuine love for design. The one thing he knows for sure is that he wants his father to be proud of him.

John's father really believes he's helping his son. His isn't trying to stifle or limit his son's future—just the opposite. He believes he's being supportive, and truly wants the best for his son. John knows this too, which is one of the reasons he's confused about what to do. If John continues down the path his father has in mind, he might have a good career, but what happens if he follows the path his father chose and ends up hating it?

The Blame Game

It's the most natural thing in the world to want someone

or something to blame when things don't work out the way we had hoped they would. When we were growing up, we had to rely on other people, and experienced situations when we felt absolutely justified holding someone else responsible for our situation. For example, before you got your driver's license your parents probably gave you many rides. It's also likely they were late sometimes, which made you late in turn. It was their fault you were late. So technically, you could blame them for making you late.

It takes a certain level of maturity to understand that sometimes things happen that no one has control over. It takes even more maturity to figure out that we're more likely to look for someone to blame when we're angry, frustrated, confused, overwhelmed, or sad about a situation. It's easier to look at other people's actions and hold them responsible for what we're experiencing. Having someone to blame helps us feel better about not having control over what happened.

Blaming other people provides access to a couple of other dangerous tendencies though—like using guilt and shame. It's a sad truth, but when people have grown up in negative situations, they do what they can to take care of themselves. Without any guidance, children learn to use what works. Many children figure out how to play the guilt card when their parents get divorced. Others try to pressure their parents with shame. Have you ever seen a child or teen make a scene in a public place to get what they want? The goal is to embarrass the parent so badly that they'll give in to the child's demands just to get them shut up.

Being able to blame other people for things that aren't working out has a limited life span though. When you were a little kid, you didn't have very much control. But with each year of your life, you are gaining control over more and more.

It's true that the longer you let people make decisions for you, the longer you get to blame them for your crummy life, but eventually time runs out. People who haven't stepped up to take charge of their own lives by then will still be angry, frustrated, moaning, and complaining; there just won't be anyone around left to blame.

The Dark Side of Blame

There's a scary side to blame too. It's when we blame ourselves for the things other people do or say. It's hard to understand how this can happen if you haven't experienced it, but there are children who grow up feeling like everything bad that happens to them or around them is their fault. Children blame themselves when their parents get divorced. Teens blame themselves when a girlfriend or a boyfriend breaks up with them. People fall under the pressure of being bullied and begin to believe it really is their fault they're being bullied.

Bullying is a situation that parents and school administrators take very seriously. But when someone calls you fat and ugly, what can you say? "Sticks and stones may break my bones but words will never hurt me?" It's a nice saying meant to help, but it doesn't. There are plenty of well-intentioned individuals who might even try to encourage the person being bullied not to take it personally. If someone you knew was being bullied, *you* might even tell them not to take it personally.

One of the reasons bullying happens is because kids are being attacked with words and actions they don't know how to defend themselves against. Their filter for defending against those words and actions hasn't fully developed yet. It may be they're too young, or they've never encountered something like this before and have no way to understand it. They might have grown up around people or situations where bullying was normal too. However it came to be, they've developed a blame filter that's ready to remind them that they are not to blame. It's all those "other people" who are to blame.

My Rotten Luck

What happens in situations when there's no one around to blame? People looking for an excuse will always find one. Take the idea of "luck." Most people are grateful when something lucky happens, but even people who consider themselves extraordinarily lucky spill their coffee, have car accidents, and catch colds at the worst possible times.

If you listen to the way people talk about luck, you'll notice luck comes into conversations when people are talking about things and situations they don't feel like they have any control over. If something turns out good, they'll say something like, "Wow; that was a lucky break" or "I really lucked out."

The reverse is the person who only sees rotten luck. If there isn't someone or something handy to blame, their blame filter is ready to blame all their problems on the mysterious force of the universe called "bad luck." They say things like, "If it weren't for bad luck, I wouldn't have any luck at all."

People who count on luck to make the difference in their lives have a hard time figuring out how to grow up, step up, and take charge of their own lives. Instead, they continue to look at the world through their blame filter, blaming Lady Luck when things don't work out.

How do you feel about luck? Here are a couple of questions for you to think about:

- What role does luck play in your life right now?
- How much of your future are you willing to turn over to luck?

It would be interesting if we could organize our lives around "good" luck, but we can't. If we could, there would be a lot more lottery winners.

Luck isn't the result of having more or less control over your life. Taking charge in an attempt to control everything won't stop bad things from happening either because bad and unfortunate things do happen. When they do, you have a few choices:

- You can give up because there's no point in trying if your "bad luck" is just going to step in and mess things up anyway.
- You can sit and wait for your luck to change (unfortunately you won't know how long it will take, or which direction it will push you).
- You can take control of your life by making decisions and taking actions that will keep you moving in the direction you want to go in, controlling what you can control regardless of luck.

It's nice when unexpected good things come your way. You can attribute them to luck if you want to, or you could accept the fact that a good thing happened while you we moving forward with your life.

How to Retire Your Blame Filter

One of the reasons a blaming filter works is because it gives us a way to deal with the emotions we have about what's happened. We get to glare at whomever or whatever is responsible for our situation, talk trash, and generally work ourselves up to believing we have every right to our feelings. But all the blaming in the world isn't going to help us get rid of all the emotion that's been building up in the meantime. Blame doesn't make it go away; most of the time it just makes it worse for us.

Have you ever noticed how much energy it takes to stay mad? Anger is one of the most toxic and taxing emotions anyone can experience. Even when you feel like your anger is totally justified, you can only keep it up for so long. The problem is that after you run out of energy, the anger is still there. It's not like you stop thinking about it either. Your thoughts turn into a loop that plays the situation over and over in your mind. It doesn't only happen with anger either. It can happen with sadness, frustration, or any other strong negative emotion. It's like you're stuck with the emotion until you can figure out how to "let it go."

And that's what people will say to you, "Oh... you just need to let it go" or "Forget about it." Who wouldn't love to be able to walk away from those feelings; but letting go is hard! It isn't easy to walk away from a situation when your emotions are still running around the inside of your head. Many times we can't get away from the people we're stuck in the situation with. They are family or friends or people we still have to interact with. Even if we're right about someone else being responsible for our situation, it's not like the person (or persons) responsible are going to step up. Sometimes, our blame filter feels like the only defense we have. As long as we keep using it, we don't have to struggle with trying to make sense of what happened on our own.

Have you ever heard the definition of insanity? Insanity is doing the same thing over and over again while expecting a different result. That's what people who make a habit of blaming others are suffering with. They believe that if they keep blaming others, they will eventually get someone to accept responsibility, and then they'll be able to let go. What they need is a way to hit the stop button long enough to realize they aren't getting anywhere. Fortunately, hitting the stop button isn't hard to do.

No one teaches us about filters, so it makes perfect sense that no one teaches us that we develop a variety of filters while we're growing up. Creating a blame filter helps us deal with the world when we feel like we don't have any control over what's happening. Small children develop a blame filter at an early age. Who hasn't heard a child say, "It's not my fault. I didn't do it. He did it!" or the favorite "That's not fair."

The childhood version of our blame filter was created with innocence. Kids are always trying to exert their control, but they don't know enough about what control is when they're very young. They don't know what it means to accept responsibility either. On the other hand, they definitely know what blame is—something to be avoided.

Most people make adjustments to their blame filter as they grow up. Some people take longer than others, while others live their entire lives holding the world accountable for their woes. As with all the filters we use to define and understand our world, the blame filter is one we don't always realize we're using. Once you learn about it though, you're in a position to stop using it. All you have to do is to start catching yourself when you're about to blame someone or something for what's going on. As soon as you start catching yourself, you're going to realize how much of your precious power you have been giving away to other people. Blame doesn't just slow us down. It leaves us at the mercy of anyone or anything that steps up to take control for us.

You might have started using a blame filter with the innocent intent of protecting yourself from getting into trouble. As you get older, if you continue to employ your blame filter, you'll limit your ability to fully embrace how much control you have over your own life. All blaming does is give more and more control to other people and situations.

Sometimes it's a struggle to let go of blaming because we literally didn't have any control over what happened. But that's the way life is sometimes. They only thing that may be absolutely true in those situations is that looking for a place to lay down blame isn't going to help you keep moving in a healthy direction.

If you don't want to get caught up in the insanity of the blame game, you need a different way to think about the situation so you can get a different result. Here are two questions to help you think differently about your situation:

1. Think about a situation where you blame (or blamed) someone for what happened to you. Is there anything that person could do or say that would resolve the situation?

If there is, then your beef with the person isn't just about what happened. It's also with the fact that they didn't care enough about you to realize how you felt about what they did. If they'd cared, they should have recognized that you were unhappy or distressed or struggling with what was happening and tried to fix it. What you really want is to hear them say they were wrong, they handled the situation poorly, or they're sorry for what happened. Any of those will work. You just want to hear them say that what happened was not your fault. In a bizarre way, blaming people is a way to keep the hope of hearing those words alive.

2. If you know you're never going to hear those words, how much more of your precious time, energy, and *life* are you willing to donate to waiting to hear them?

We may not always get the answers we want, but it's a mistake to believe we need other people's permission or validation to move on. Every minute you spend waiting is a minute you don't get to spend doing something you enjoy with people you enjoy being with and around—people who do genuinely care about you.

Letting go isn't about forgiveness either. People can and do things we might never be able to forgive. Letting go is simply about realizing that sitting and waiting for the past to change is a waste of time. What happened in the past is never going to change no matter how hard you try to change it.

If you want your situation to change, do it by taking control of what you can control—yourself. In the end, the blame filter is simply about excuses. It's okay when we're kids, but it's another thing we can leave behind along with all the other things we've outgrown.

Flexing Your Filters:

One of the reasons these exercises are here is because a book like this is going to make you aware of things you weren't aware of before you read it. This chapter might have you thinking about how many people you blame for things that have happened to you. You might be absolutely correct about some of them too. There are definitely times when other people are to blame for our circumstances.

In the space provided, start by listing five situations where you blamed someone for something that happened to you. Then, for each situation, consider the two questions leading to this exercise, and write down which result would have made a difference for you.

1. _____

_____

_____

2. _____

_____

_____

3. _____

_____

_____

4. _____

_____

_____

5. _____

_____

_____

On the following lines, write down five situations where you feel like you have control over what's happening. See if you can identify what it is that you have control over, and what it is about that aspect of control that matters most to you. As it is with all of these exercises and questions, there are no right or wrong answers. They are just opportunities for you to learn more about yourself.

1. _____

_____

2. _____

_____

3. _____

_____

4. _____

_____

5. _____

_____

3

Competition

Once you make the decision to stop relying on your blame filter, you're in an interesting situation. At first it's like trying to break a habit. It would be easier if everybody around you would cooperate and stop doing what they're doing, but they won't. You will still be dealing with the same people at school, at work, at home, and socially. In most cases, the only person who will know about your decision is you.

At first it can be a little frightening because you're giving up one of your "go-to" responses. On the other hand, it can be eye opening. You'll be looking at people without all that predetermined blaming energy. Add your new knowledge that everybody is viewing their world through one of their own filters, and you'll start seeing people differently.

For one thing, you'll notice that you aren't the only person struggling with relationships. Being able to successfully handle relationships and the challenges they present is something we all have to figure out. The conflicts we experience while we're trying to figure them out are a normal part of the process, especially when personalities and personal agendas clash. Nobody likes relationship hassles, but people are people and that makes hassles inevitable.

Right now, learning about filters gives you a distinct advantage. When you see conflict between two people, you'll know that each person is viewing the situation through their own filter. From each person's perspective, there is one solution to the conflict that's better than the other—theirs.

Isn't that everyone's position though? We don't get into arguments or conflicts when we agree about how things are going. We get into them when someone or something has gotten between us and what we want.

Because our filters only work one way, it's easy to forget that the person/people on the other side of a conflict are doing the exact same thing we are—looking at the world through a filter's perspective. We can't look through their filter and see what's influencing their actions. They can't look through our filter to understand where we're coming from either. We can speculate, but if the wrong filter is in place, it will interfere with our ability to speculate with kindness, empathy, and genuine concern.

We all know what this feels like. It's stressful and uncomfortable to be in the position of looking at someone and realizing the other person doesn't seem to care about us, or what's going on with us. It could be the reverse too. Maybe we're the one who's gotten so focused on getting our way that all we see is an obstacle between us and what we want. In both cases the result is the same; our competitive filter gets triggered.

Your Competitive Filter

This filter comes into play when you're not ready to back down or give up your position. Instead, you dig your heels in and stand your ground until you win, or something happens to change the situation and you decide you don't care what happens anymore.

A competitive filter is great for when we're actually competing. We can use it to block out distractions so we can stay focused on the task at hand. It puts us in "warrior" mode, and helps us remain calm and clear about what we need to do to achieve our goal. To get the most out of our competition filter though, we have to put our emotions on hold.

That's why a competitive filter doesn't work well when it comes to conflicts, disagreements, and conflicting agendas. These are not true contests or competitions. They are emotionally charged situations that tend to block out thoughts of how important or meaningful "winning" is—or isn't. Once we're in competition mode, we want what we want. It happens. Just about everybody has thrown at least one friend under the bus when they've been under the influence of their competitive filter.

You've probably experienced the other side of it too... people looking to create conflict by pushing your buttons until they hit the one that gets you to react. If someone's bugging you and won't stop, it might be because they're glaring at you through their competitive filter, trying to get you engaged in their game. You know what happens next. They keep pushing until they push the right button and you're competition filter finally answers the call.

Fortunately, your competitive filter works like any other filter. Once you're aware of its presence, you'll start getting better at figuring out when it's a good filter to use (like when you're in a genuine competition) and when it's more likely to get in the way. It will be easier to recognize other people's dramas for what they are, and you'll be less likely to get sucked into situations where people are just trying to get you riled up.

Your awareness isn't likely to stop other people from trying to get you to respond, or from throwing you under the bus if you don't respond. But at least you'll have another way to understand what happened. And the truth is, if someone's willing to throw you under the bus to "win," then the situation wasn't about you anyway. It was all about them and what they decided they wanted or needed. Their competitive filter interfered with their ability to see you as a person. You were simply the obstacle in the way.

Embracing this truth won't make the hurtful and harmful things people say or do more acceptable. It will provide you with the freedom to not take other people's actions as a direct threat to who you are as a person. Start paying attention to the ways you react in those situations. At the very least, it will make it easier to mentally step away. Remember, it takes at least two people to create a conflict. You don't have to agree to be one of them.

So What Does This Mean for You?

At some point in this process you'll start recognizing that everybody is dealing with something. Think about what the people around you are dealing with on a daily basis. After all, they're getting up to go to school or work too. They have families to take care of. They're concerned about their careers and how—or if—they're going to succeed. The better we become at recognizing how our actions are affected by the filters we use, the more understanding and insight we'll gain into the ways other people use their filters.

Everyone has a collection of filters they use to view the world through. They are developed by life experiences, personality, upbringing, and wants and needs. Most people aren't aware that their perspectives are influenced by their filters. They believe their words and actions are justified because there's something in their head telling them their actions are justified.

"I'm dealing drugs right now because I don't have any other options," or "If I'm not hard on my kids now, they won't be tough enough to handle what the world will throw at them later." Phrases like these are spoken every day, month after month, year after year. Whatever someone is doing, no matter how destructive it seems, some form of justification exists within their minds.

It's important to acknowledge that the filters we use aren't inherently good or bad. One individual might have been raised in a way that encouraged them to look through their competitive filter to find the weaknesses in others. But our world is full of athletes, politicians, leaders, parents, and teenagers who use their competitive filter to help others recognize what's possible. They show us how much we are capable of, and remind us that the only limits we have are the ones we place on ourselves. When they help another person, it's because they believe it's the right thing to do. They could have gone in the other direction, deciding they were better than those below them, but they didn't. Instead of using their words or deeds to keep any potential competition down, they extended a hand and helped raise them up.

This means that you can let go of believing that the things people do or say to you are because of you. They aren't. We can be part of a situation, we can even do something that makes a situation worse; it doesn't matter. You have a choice about what to do, and so does everybody else involved. When people do things, they do them for reasons that are locked away in their own mind.

We do like to speculate though. We might even believe we can figure out why the people we like—or don't like—do what they do. We want to understand the people we care about so we can be there for them and help them if they need it. Parents feel this way when their teenagers start screaming at them for no obvious reason. They could take it personally and start screaming right back. Thankfully, most parents don't.

With people we aren't comfortable around, it's tricky because there's a part of us always wondering what it is we're doing wrong. We want to know what motivated someone else's actions so we can let go of the idea that we are the cause of their actions.

Years ago, I started having difficulties working with a colleague I didn't know very well. This gentleman was professional, prestigious, and well respected, so it was a surprise to me when he began blaming me for things that were going wrong with a project we were both working on. Before long, he was being really tough on me and generally making my life difficult.

I asked myself, "Why is this happening? He doesn't even know me." Like most people, I wanted to understand what was going on. I wanted to know if it was because of something I was doing, or because that was the way he was. I could have confronted him, but I wasn't ready for that. Instead, I decided to take a step back and spend some time thinking and analyzing the situation from different perspectives. I also had a confidential conversation with someone we both worked with hoping to get some insight from someone else's perspective.

I hit the same stumbling blocks everybody in a situation like this deals with—there was no way for me to know why without asking him. I couldn't *make* him like me, or ask other people to talk to him and tell him why he should like me. It was a contest I couldn't win. It was also a contest I didn't want to participate in. The only thing I could do was to stop taking it personally and approach him as a colleague and someone I had respect for in the hope that he would do the same.

So I talked to him. I simply made a point of getting to know my colleague and allowing him to get to know me. I guess you could say I "killed him with kindness," taking my own advice on understanding that everybody views the world through their own filters and from their own perspective. I made a conscious decision not to approach him like this was a popularity contest I could win if I could figure out what he wanted. There was no guarantee I was going to get the result I hoped for with this approach either. But I was willing to try, and over time, we became good friends at work.

How Deep Should You Dig for Understanding?

It's easy to build a case against someone. Easy to justify why we don't like someone or why they don't like us. We can say, "He doesn't like me because he's jealous of my position at work," or, "I can't stand her, she's too quiet." It could be anything, but it boils down to trying to find some piece of evidence that puts us in a position to get what we want. It may not sound like competition, but any situation that has an inkling of one-upmanship is competitive.

With my colleague, I could have taken a different route. I could have drilled everybody who knew him to piece together the puzzle of who this man was and what his motivations were. I could have wasted hours and hours of my life coming up with all kinds of speculations and making assumptions about him based solely on the way he was treating me. But what would those actions have accomplished? At the end of all that wasted time and energy, I still wouldn't know him. He still wouldn't know me either. And our relationship still wouldn't be good.

The problem with speculations and assumptions is that we can start to believe them simply because they seem to make sense on the surface. We talk them over with our friends, they agree, and then suddenly we're so caught up with our ideas that we start treating people as if we know the private and personal motivations framing their perspectives. How would you feel if someone did that to you?

What you want to develop is the ability to understand that people are always being influenced by their motivations. Your goal shouldn't be to discover someone else's actual motivations. How many of your friends know the secrets of all your motivations right now? I'm willing to bet there's at least one big motivation you haven't shared with all your friends. And yet that one motivation could be influencing your perspective more than any other.

We don't need to know why people do everything. Again, if you become focused on the why, it could be because you're trying to figure out where you fit into the picture. When you start building a relationship with another person, you don't start by asking them their deepest and darkest secrets. You start by being nice and talking.

Our days are filled with interactions. Sure, we could hide in a cave in an attempt to avoid relationship stress, but would that really solve the problem? The reality of our world is that there will always be people in our lives we will never get along with. It could be a family member, a peer, a student, or someone we work with. It doesn't matter. Just step back and think about which one of your filters might be influencing your experience in that situation.

Don't fall back on your blaming filter. Remind yourself that it isn't personal, even when it feels like it is. Ask yourself if there is an element of competition, and be honest with the answer. Competition comes in many disguises, but it always contains some element of proving yourself. If you realize your competition filter has been triggered, shift your focus away from thinking about why someone did what they did. Put your thinking cap on and figure out what you have control over.

Figuring out the filters you've been using by default is an interesting process. It's very freeing too. Before you started learning about them you might have felt like you didn't have any control over your life, and that life and relationships were a competition you weren't any good at. Now you know the reverse. With a little awareness and practice, you will become more confident about the things you do and say.

Flexing Your Filters:

This exercise is to help you understand more about how your competitive filter might be influencing your actions. Start by listing three times when you got mad at someone for something they did that made it impossible for you to get what you wanted. Write down who it was, and what you didn't get as a result.

1. _____
_____
_____

2. _____
_____
_____

3. _____
_____
_____

It is so easy to become competitive. So easy in fact that most people don't even realize when it's happening. There's nothing wrong with being competitive either—unless you take your losses too seriously.

Take another look at each of the situations you just listed from a competition perspective. Did you lose your temper? If you did, can you think back and maybe come up with some ideas for a better way to deal with the situation if it comes up again?

1. _____

_____

_____

2. _____

_____

_____

3. _____

_____

_____

_____

At the very least, owning the fact that we all have a competitive filter is one way to increase the odds that you won't embarrass yourself the next time things don't go as you had hoped or planned.

4

A Sense of Self

Once you start taking control of the temptation to blame other people for what's going on, and have started recognizing how easy it is to get caught up in competition, something very interesting happens. There's more room to think about what you want to have happen. Both blaming and competition are reactions. We blame people as a reaction to what they've done. Feeling like we have to fight or compete for what we want is a reaction too. When we don't waste as much of our time reacting, we have more opportunities to choose how we want to act. We get to make decisions based on our own goals, desires, beliefs, passions, likes, and dislikes. This is when our sense-of-self filter truly starts to take shape.

As you've probably realized, filters are not permanent fixtures. In fact, they can be very flexible and adaptable, and that's a good thing. We can realize we've been looking through a filter that hasn't been doing us any favors and decide not to use it anymore. We can choose to develop filters too, like filters that will help us recognize opportunities for kindness and generosity. Developing an awareness of the filters we use to view the world through can definitely improve the quality of our life. And so it is with our sense-of-self filter.

We all know what a sense of self is—in theory. It's that sense of knowing exactly how you feel about yourself that develops as we make decisions about the kind person we believe we are (or believe we want to be). It's the result of choices and decisions we've made about what we believe about life, and about what's important not just to us, but to the world too. Our sense of self helps us claim our place in the world.

No one can see our sense of self either. It's one of the most private and personal aspects of who we are, and that's one of the reasons why our sense of self is so vulnerable. When people look at us, they see an "identity." They see a person, male or female, young or old, blonde or brunette, etc. They don't know us through our sense of self. They get to know us through our actions. If we scowl all the time, they'll probably think we're grumpy all the time. If we smile all the time, they'll probably think we're happy all the time. People's assumptions may be right or wrong, but it doesn't matter. Only we know what's behind our smiles and frowns.

It's not like our sense of self suddenly kicks in and we run around shouting, "This is who I am! How do you like me now!" either. There are people who live their lives like this though. Politicians do it when they're running for office. Artists, musicians, actors, dancers, and athletes often display their sense of self through their work. But for most of us, the thought of exposing who we are to the world is too scary. We just don't have enough confidence to do it. And the less confidence we have, the more vulnerable our sense of self is.

By the same token, the more our confidence grows, the stronger our sense of self becomes. We all know what that looks like from the outside too. It's the person who doesn't seem to be as bothered when other people have different opinions, ideas, or beliefs.

Imposing Imposters

There is however, one situation you need to be aware of—the ways some people will try to shape and mold your sense of self by imposing their opinions, beliefs, and truths on you while you're still trying to develop your own opinions, beliefs, and truths.

It almost doesn't seem possible that other people could impose limits on a filter, but it happens all the time. People will try to get you to accept that their view of the world is better than yours. Sometimes they honestly believe they're seeing what's really going on (even if they can't explain why they believe it's true) and sincerely believe you're problem is that you can't see the truth. These people can get very focused on what they believe, and are often prone to pulling out all the stops to get you to accept their "truth."

Sometimes it's not really a big deal. Every teenager has experienced this kind of determined thinking from an ordinary perspective, such as when they make the decision that it's no longer okay for a parent to buy clothes for them. Or when they decide to listen to a different type of music than what they grew up hearing. If you look at those two situations from the perspective of the sense-of-self filter, it's easy to see there isn't one right or wrong truth or belief about clothes or music. It's simply about our sense-of-self filter making decisions about who we are becoming in terms of our tastes.

As our sense-of-self filter is developing, it's not always easy to make the big decisions about what we think, feel, and believe. Like all our filters, this one develops over time, and one of the challenges we face during that time is figuring out what to do when our sense of self doesn't agree with someone else's opinion about who we should be. Who's right? Should we stick to our thoughts about who we are no matter what? Or should we give up our view in favor of someone else's?

The answers to questions like those always start with remembering that most people don't realize they're viewing the world through a filter. Again, they think they're seeing truth. So when someone looks at us, they might believe they know what's best. Once you acknowledge that this might be the case, deciding what to do next requires some thought. For example, what would you do if your best friend's sense of self suddenly altered to include the belief that getting drunk is okay? If the person is really your best friend, you have a tricky choice to make. Whose filter are you going to view the world through now? Are you going to stick to your filter—the one with the belief that getting drunk isn't okay? Or are you going to alter your sense of self and embrace the idea that getting drunk is okay so that you're once again in alignment with your friend's filter?

The hardest part of a situation like this isn't answering the question about whether or not it's okay to get drunk. The hard part is realizing that your answer might forever alter the relationship you have with your best friend. If you chose your sense-of-self filter, the relationship may end. But even if you pretend to choose your friend's belief so you can still be friends, will your friendship ever be the same again?

When Your Opinion Doesn't Matter

An even tougher situation is when the person trying to impose their view on you isn't interested in anything you have to say. In some cases, they aren't even giving you a choice about adopting their view. When you're in school, people might call this peer pressure, but this kind of pressure isn't limited to school, and everybody experiences it at different times in their lives.

It would be great to be able to tell you this won't happen to you, and that you'll be able to create a life without coming in contact with people who will try their hardest to impose their beliefs on you, but I can't. Most people will respect your views and ideas, but there are going to be people and situations where that won't be the case. When you find yourself in one of those situations, your previous experience is likely to be a huge determining factor.

The younger a person is, the less likely they are to have anywhere near enough confidence to stand up for themselves. Even if they did have the confidence, that's not how most of us were raised. We weren't raised to defend ourselves against our elders, or people in a position of power. We were raised to listen and do what people told us to do (and believe). When we were young, if we asked why we were expected to do something, we heard things like, "It's for your own good" and "Because I said so."

As soon as we start developing "a mind of our own," it gets complicated so we start developing our sense-of-self filter to will help us sort out how and when it's okay to disagree, or take a different path. When our attempts to grow hit resistance, at some point, our natural instinct to defend ourselves will kick in and start exerting itself.

If you were to stop and think about it right now, could you think of someone in your life who isn't acknowledging the fact that you've decided who you are as a person, and instead just keeps trying to impose their views on you regardless of what you say? How frustrating is that?! Every teenager has experienced this with a parent, but that's to be expected, it's part of growing up and becoming your own person. But what about people you've encountered in school? Isn't this what bullies do—regardless of how old they are—impose their view of the world on others without any regard for another's thoughts or feelings?

There's no age limit for bullying, and no age limit for being frustrated, angry, or annoyed when someone treats you like you aren't capable of making a decision on our own, or that any decision you make is wrong or irrelevant. The one thing that helps us get over hurdles like these is life experience. Think back to the people who didn't seem to care about what you thought or felt. Can you remember what it felt like not having enough experience to know how to stand up for yourself?

The less experience someone has, the more likely their first responses will be to avoid saying or doing anything because they don't want the situation to get any worse than it already is. Without any positive interactions to balance it out, they might start developing a sense-of-self filter that defends their right to take a stand and respond by blowing up and attacking the other person's view. Unchecked, the adult version of this could be the person who constantly talks-up the value of their point of view while devaluing the points of view of others, without making any kind of an attempt to understand where someone else is coming from.

On the other hand, experiencing positive results with early attempts at expressing who we think we are can help our sense of self develop. As we respond to challenges and get good results, we gain insight that helps our confidence grow. As adults, these are people who can acknowledge that we all have a point of view without feeling the need to impose their "rightness" on someone else. When they encounter people who try to impose their personal views on them, they can listen without feeling intimidated, and even let what's being said go in one ear and out the other when it's necessary.

We all struggle with trying to figure out how to defend our thoughts and beliefs from the challenges other people present us with. But again, as we continue to grow, we learn from our experiences and begin to recognize more truths about what it means to be human. We don't have to agree with everybody. There are usually multiple ways to view specific situations. Everybody is entitled to their own viewpoint too.

There are other insights we get exposed to too, such as the truth that we don't have to convince anyone that our view of the world is better than someone else's. We don't have to share the same view of the world as our family, friends, neighbors, or co-workers either. People can view the world through a completely different sense of self and still respect each other and treat each other with respect. Remember that we cannot control other people. We can only control how we think and feel. And that means that each of us truly has the right to decide who we want to be.

Flexing Your Filters:

We talked a lot about confidence in this chapter, but confidence is not a filter. Confidence is a result. The more positive results we experience as we attempt things, the more confidence we have. When it comes to our sense-of-self filter, our confidence isn't always obvious. Many times it's hidden just below the surface. Becoming more confident happens when we look below the surface and discover times when we acted confidently.

In this exercise, come up with five situations when something you thought, felt, or believed about yourself was being challenged. For example, maybe you and a friend decide to go to the movies. When you get to the theatre, your friend changes his/her mind and decides they want to see the new horror flick which is rated R. You and your friend had originally agreed to see the new action adventure that's rated PG. Your friend looks at you and says, "Come on. That movie is for kids and losers." Yes, it sounds like a small thing... and it's not like your friend is actually calling you a *kid* or a *loser*, but it could be a challenge to your sense of self—especially if horror flicks totally creep you out.

With each situation you think of, write about the challenge, and how you responded. There isn't a right or wrong answer here either. This is just an exercise you can use to identify a few times when you had the confidence to be true to your sense of self. You'll probably identify times when a lack of confidence meant you "caved" too. If that's the case, now would be a great time to think about what you might do if a similar situation pops up in the future.

A Sense of Self

1. _____
_____
_____
_____
_____

2. _____
_____
_____
_____
_____

3. _____
_____
_____
_____
_____

4. _____
_____
_____
_____
_____

5. _____
_____
_____
_____
_____

.

5

Role Models

Thank goodness we have a world full of role models to choose from. How crazy would it be if our filters developed solely as the result of our interactions with parents, relatives, and teachers, and that was it!? First of all, we'd all end up pinched into a small range of expression simply because no one would ever think outside the box they grew up in. Second of all, no one would grow. We'd all be taught what to think, do, and be when we were kids, and that would be it.

Outside the Box

Every contribution to our world is the result of someone expanding their filters to embrace the truth that something else might be possible beyond what people currently think or believe. People who expand their filters expand their view of what might be possible too. They push through their own limits—and sometimes everyone else's limits. People like Aristotle, Einstein, Martin Luther King, Oprah, and John Walsh are all examples of people who started by making the decision that it would be okay to explore the world beyond their current limits. And yet they had to grow up and develop their filters just like we do. They could have given into the comfort, security, and predictability of living inside the same box as all the well-intentioned adults around them had been living in for most of their lives, but they didn't. None of those people was content to look through the same predetermined filters the people around them used and simply emulate that lifestyle for the rest of their lives.

Some people might say those individuals were courageous... they felt the fear and did it anyway... but the truth is that we all have the ability to *feel the fear and do it anyway*. In fact, we're born with it. Anyone who's ever heard a baby screaming at the top of their tiny lungs knows this to be true. It might not always be easy to figure out what they want, but they're trying their hardest to let us know what it is.

When we're babies, we don't wait to express ourselves, we just do it. But as we grow, we start feeling the pressure of the people around us starting to limit our attempts to express ourselves. They start influencing and shaping our filters with their interpretations of the difference between acceptable and unacceptable thoughts, behaviors, and actions, and with each passing day, our filters become more defined.

But, when you look around, you'll notice something really interesting. There are people who were brought up in incredibly strict surroundings who grew to become true adventurers. And there are people who grew up with all the freedom and encouragement anyone could possibly hope for who grew up content to stay within the confines of a box even narrower than the one they were raised in.

What Just Happened?

We either grow into, or grow out of the filters we started developing as children. Much of the time it happens naturally.

Like the day you decided you weren't going to wear "little kid" clothes anymore. One day they were okay to wear, the next day they weren't.

Our ability to think matures. As it does, we start filtering out the ways a "kid" would do something, replacing those child-like views with more adult-like views of the world. We make adjustments to our filters when new situations and information introduce us to new ways of looking at the world that are different than what we've been told and taught. For the most part, this is an exciting process of discovery. But there are also situations when our developing filters are truly challenged. Remember when you used to believe in the Tooth Fairy and the Easter Bunny?

Sure, it's easy to laugh at it now, but the moment we realize that the people we trusted didn't always tell us the truth, things change. It doesn't matter whether they had our best intentions at heart either. It's still a dilemma, and now we have a reason to wonder about all the other things people have taught us or shared with us. Sometimes we even come to a complete stop because the filters we've been developing and relying on to make sense of our world suddenly don't feel or fit right.

Imagine a filter as being like a contact lens. What would happen to your ability to see the world around you if a section of the lens was suddenly at the wrong prescription? Even if you tried to look around the problem, or to ignore it, it would still be interfering with your ability to see your world clearly. That's what it's like when one or more our filters is challenged by something that doesn't fit or feel right. Once it's happens, it's happened. We can't go back in time and make it *un-happen*.

We've all experienced this too. It's like one moment

everything is working, and then the next it isn't. One day you had everything in common with a friend, and then the next day you didn't. One day you thought you had your future all planned out, and the next all you can see in your future is a huge black hole.

Sometimes challenges to our filters happen so quickly that it feels like we've just been hit with a sucker punch, and we're at a complete loss of what to do. It's a very different experience than the experience of updating our filters. When we're updating, all we're doing is replacing old thoughts and ideas that are no longer relevant to us with new thoughts and ideas that are. For example, when you decided to start dressing more like an adult, you just updated your filter by deleting the idea that you wanted to dress like a cool kid, and updated it with a view of yourself dressed more like a cool adult.

Sudden challenges aren't always easy to deal with. We rarely have anything to immediately replace what's just been lost, and now there's a gaping hole in our filter that every part of our being will feel compelled to fill. To fill the hole, we start looking around—sometimes frantically—for something or someone else that seems like a good fit. Chances are very good the person or people responsible for our situation aren't going to be on the top of our "go to for advice" list either. Chances are much better we're going to search for someone who looks like they've already solved the problem we're experiencing, and are living the life we'd like to be living right now. This is one of the reasons why so many kids turn to gangs. They are looking for that family, that connection to be cared about, to belong, and to feel like they're valued.

It can be tricky to make decisions about who to look up to when we don't have a lot of life experience yet. Trickier still when we're trying to fill a hole, or fix something inside that feels broken. More often than not, we'll follow our heart. That's not always a bad decision, but sometimes it limits what we see. Hearts move quickly, sometimes blindly, and we might miss the whole picture as a result.

In times of need, we might not care about all the other stuff going on in the life of someone we're looking up to. And there are definitely times when we deliberately avoid looking at the whole picture. We just figure we're only going to emulate one aspect of someone's life, so that's what we focus on, ignoring all the rest. Sometimes it's less stressful to look up to someone who's living a life that's the exact opposite of our life right now, a life that's as far away from our life as we could possibly imagine. It's easier to focus on what we need to see—someone who appears to have everything we want. Looking up to them helps us believe there's hope for us.

How Do You Know?

It's not all that easy to figure out who would be a good role model. But if you take a minute to look at some of the role models the adults around you have, you'll immediately recognize that even people with a lot of life experience have questionable role models. Life experience is only one aspect of our choice.

If you take the term "role model" literally, role models are people living a role you could choose to model. A role model is a person looked up to by others as an example to be imitated—or not. There are good role models and bad role models, and we see just as many people in our lives that we don't want to emulate as those we do. While we're growing up, all the people around us are in a position to influence us, especially people in positions of authority and trust. Fortunately for us, we can learn from both the good and the bad role models we have in our lives.

There aren't any restrictions on who can be a role model either. Anyone can be a role model. They don't have to be related, or famous, or someone we know. Role models aren't required to be good or bad people. Role models are just people who have something, or are doing something we wish we could have or do for ourselves.

Role models play an important role in our lives though. If we didn't have them, how would we ever know there are different ways of living and being in the world? Role models can definitely influence and challenge our filters too, but most of the time there's enough distance in the relationship between us and our role models that it's a one-way deal.

For example, a musician can challenge you to expand the filter you use to decide what qualifies as great music. An author can challenge you to think about your beliefs. Politicians can challenge you to decide how involved you want to be in the politics of your school and/or community. All of these people can become role models for you and influence the filters you use to make future choices, but chances are you will know more about them than they know about you.

Role models aren't limited to people who have status. Brothers, sisters, mothers, fathers, grandparents, ministers, and teachers can all be role models. Nor do we choose our role models just as a way to rebel (although just about every teenager has been told by a parent that that's what they're doing). We usually choose our role models because they have something in their life that we don't, or because they have something in their life we'd like to use as a replacement for what we have in our life right now.

Who Will You Look Up To?

Role models aren't just a source of opportunity for growth, success, or fun. Role models can be lifeboats too. When our lives fall apart we instinctively look for help. We don't just look up to role models because they look better than us, we choose them because they aren't us. It doesn't always matter how much we actually have in common with the role models we choose either. We might look up to someone simply because they survived what we're currently going through.

The most important thing about role models is to understand that they have a "whole" life. The life we see is usually just a portion of the life they live. So when you're looking at someone and thinking about how nice it would be to be like them, remind yourself that just because someone is doing their best to look happy, that doesn't mean they are. People who have the big house, the fancy car, and the fat bank account aren't always as successful and happy as they appear, and emulating them might lead to playing out other scenarios in their life that are better avoided.

The reality is that our role models experience challenges to their filters just like we do. Being famous or beautiful or popular or rich doesn't mean their life is automatically better than the life of one of the "little people." Yes, they may own a big house and a nice car, but if they're spending time in rehab every year, things are definitely different inside their house than they appear to be from the outside. Is spending time in rehab something you're hoping to do too? Of course it isn't.

But it's easy to overlook that part of their life because that's what "friends" do.

Obviously, there are role models who are better for us than others, and I don't mean to pick on those who are famous. But famous or not, there are people who stand out from the crowd, and there is something about their lives we are drawn to like magnets regardless of what else is going on with them.

We follow the antics and adventures of our role models, and believe we understand the struggles they've had to overcome to get to where they are now. We feel a connection with them and believe they would know exactly how we're feeling without us having to explain it to them. Just knowing they're there gives us hope that we can get through our struggles too.

We don't just look up to them because their life looks better than ours either. We look because it helps us forget about our life right now. Why would we choose to look for their problems when we'd just as soon avoid looking at our own?

Choosing Who to Carpe Diem With

When you think about it, just about everyone in your life is a role model once in a while. Everyone you think about and interact with is giving you some type of feedback about your life. We grow up trusting those people because that's what's expected of us, and we make choices and decisions based on their reactions, opinions, and advice. Wouldn't it make sense to figure out if they're a good or bad role model? Here are some questions to consider:

- How are the people in my life different from each other?
- What direction is each person headed in?
- What kinds of results are they getting with what they're doing?
- If there was one thing I would change about each person's life, what would it be?

Truly good role models are people living the lives they really want—not the lives other people want. They are who they want to be. When you're evaluating the people in your life, try to figure out if they're truly happy, or just pretending that everything's fine. Do you really want what they have, not just in a material sense, but also what's inside of them? Are they really at peace? Do their lives reflect clarity and meaning?

Motivational speaker Jim Rohn once said that "success leaves clues." He was right. There are repeatable patterns of behavior more likely to lead to success. The same goes for failure too—there are repeatable patterns of behavior more likely to lead to failure. This is a good thing because it means we have choices.

Even without a lot of life experience, we can make choices and decisions about what we do and don't want in our life. To start building an amazing life, start by thinking about the things you want to do and be and feel (even when you're struggling). It's easy to skip this step and instead replace it with looking at what a role model has and make the decision that if it's good enough for them, it's good enough for us. But remember, we're not talking about emulating someone's life in a literal sense.

For example, a teenager could choose LeBron James as a

role model and diligently try to follow in the footsteps of his success. But if he is only 5'5" tall, it's highly unlikely he's going to become a power forward in the NBA. If he starts his quest by trying to be LeBron, at some point he'd be forced to give up simply because he wasn't tall enough.

If our "short" NBA-inspired guy had started his quest by thinking about the qualities, attitudes, and attributes that led to Lebron's success, he would have dramatically improved his own chances for success. For one thing, he would have acknowledged he was too short on his own rather than wait for someone else to do it for him. Being short doesn't mean he has to give up his dream of being part of the NBA either. He could become a famous reporter, or an on-air celebrity who focuses on the NBA, or a winning and inspiring coach.

Starting out by trying to emulate a role model's success *exactly,* rarely pays off. Your role models aren't going to be around to set your alarm clock so you get up early to study, or work out, or cook a good breakfast. People like LeBron probably didn't have anyone doing those things for them either. The role models he chose left enough clues for him to keep moving in the right direction. After that, it was up to him to do what was necessary to keep closing the distance between where he was and where he wanted to be.

Do You Know Who Your Role Models Are?

Your instinct might be to say yes, but think about this for a minute. When people are growing up, their first role models were the people they spent the most time with, whether that was a parent, relative, caretaker, teacher, or guardian. When you look back, were all those people good role models for you? Or have you already begun to recognize things about those people you didn't see when you were younger—like relatives you thought were funny until you were old enough to realize they were alcoholics, abusive, emotionally unstable, or all three!

How are those people doing now? Are they leading happy lives? Do they seem like people who are clear about where they want to go? Are they taking action to make their dreams come true? What kinds of thoughts, beliefs, and ideas do you think their filters are composed of?

Bad role models can have just as profound an effect on us when we're growing up as the good ones—sometimes more. This is especially true for people who've grown up around physical and psychological abuse, anger, and/or substance abuse and never seem to escape the negative cycles that continue to play out generation after generation within their family. It's easy to blame it all on genetics with statements like, "I inherited my mom's/father's temper" or "My mom/dad couldn't stop drinking either."

The reality is that a huge majority of those behaviors are learned as the result of seeing and hearing them being repeated over and over and over again. When that's all that's available to you, it can have a huge impact on the way your filters develop.

Embracing Your Path

Fortunately, none of us is doomed to follow in the footsteps of the bad role models we've had in our life. Often times, the only reason they're still in our lives is because we've become so used to their presence that we don't realize how much they're influencing our choices and decisions. In other words, they've become a habit.

Habits provide us with the security of predictability. It doesn't matter if they are good or bad habits either, our habits group together to create our comfort zones. That's all a comfort zone is... a collection of behaviors that have turned into habits that don't require any active thinking on our part. When we're in our comfort zones, we aren't challenged to think about how our lives are progressing. Unfortunately, the result of this can be living out the same situations, falling back on the same behaviors with the same people and the same role models, day after day for the rest of our lives!

Comfort zones may feel safe, but your chances of moving in a different direction grow slimmer as time passes. Breaking the cycle starts with simply realizing that even a role model may be nothing more than a habit.

When I counsel students about where to go to school, I often advise that they go away to college so they can get away from all the role models and expectations they've grown up with. Going away puts them in the position of being able to see and experience a new group of people and all the different things those people think and do. It's the experience that helps them gather information they can use to start defining what they want their lives to be like. Too many kids don't see enough good role models in their lives, and the ones they think might be good, might only be good in the short-run.

Obviously, going away to school isn't the only option. The world is full of positive role models for you to observe. We live in "global" times and that means you can even have role models who live on the other side of the planet. There are plenty of amazing historical role models worthy of our admiration and respect for all they accomplished too.

However you choose to do it, just remember that the more information you gather about the kinds of lives being lived around you, the more information you'll have when deciding what kind of life you want for yourself. If you don't allow yourself to be exposed to anything beyond what you grew up with, then you won't be as likely to pick up on other people's patterns of behavior. On the other hand, your confidence in the filters you're using to interact with the world will grow as you develop your ability to recognize that the decisions other people make come through their own personal filters too.

Learning from others is a great way to save the time and emotion of going through every experience personally. There's an old expression that says, "A fool doesn't learn from his own mistakes. A smart man does learn from his own mistakes, but a wise man learns from other people's mistakes." I want you to learn from other people's mistakes so that you can avoid them altogether.

Comfort zones are a nice idea, but they can limit your opportunities by limiting the people and situations you're exposed to. Over time, you might actually start believing that anything outside your comfort zone is wrong, or frightening, or a situation to be avoided at all costs. Your first instinct might be to say that that will never happen to you, but there are probably people in your life right now who avoid anything that's *different*. And I'm sure you've heard the phrase "Don't rock the boat." Is that how you're envisioning your future?

Flexing Your Filters:

Think of three **bad** role models who play—or have played—a part in your life. Write down two things about each that first grabbed your attention, and then write down how those things have influenced the way you live your life now.

1. _____

_____

_____

_____

_____

_____

_____

2. _____

_____

_____

_____

_____

_____

3. _____

_____

_____

_____

_____

_____

Think of three **good** role models who play—or have played—a part in your life. For each one, write down two things you admire about them, and one decision you've made about your own life as a result.

1. _____

_____

_____

_____

_____

_____

_____

2. _____

_____

_____

_____

_____

_____

3. _____

_____

_____

_____

_____

_____

Think of yourself as a role model for someone in your future. (Maybe you have a younger brother or sister at home?) What two qualities would you hope someone would be inspired to emulate from your life. What one piece of advice would you give that someone if they were to aspire to follow in your footsteps?

Quality #1
_____
_____
_____

Quality #2
_____
_____
_____

Your Advice:
_____
_____
_____

6

Fear Doesn't Always Have to be Scary

On the surface, fear seems like a pretty simple thing. It's very primal, and its basic job is to keep us safe. In the days of the caveman when there were plenty of things to be fearful of, fear helped people react quickly and do what they needed to do to stay alive. Obviously, our world is safer now, but we still rely on fear to keep us safe—like when it gets a driver to react quickly by slamming on their car's breaks so they don't hit the car in front of them, or when a parent grabs their child's hand before he/she touches a hot stove.

Fear is also a very natural response to situations when we don't understand what's going on. Parts of our brain are programmed to always be looking for anything that might be a threat to our safety and well-being. As soon as our senses catch a glimpse of anything it isn't sure of, it doesn't wait around for our thinking mind to catch up. Instead, our brains respond by pumping us full of things like adrenaline so we can react quickly and do what we have to do to keep ourselves safe.

It's great that our body does this for us because it lets us pay attention to all the other stuff going on around us. Sometimes though, our body's response is so quick that it makes mistakes—like when we're in bed at night, in the dark, staring at the wall, and we're convinced we see a huge spider moving around. Our heart starts racing and we reach for the light switch as quickly as we can. Then we see that the spider is actually just a weird spot on the wall that's been there forever.

We all know what it feels like to be afraid, but we all experience fear differently. We're not all afraid of the same things either. You might be afraid of heights while your friend can't wait to climb to the top of the highest mountain.

Fear can be a double-edged sword. Yes, it can generate a genuine life-saving response, but it can also make us afraid of everyday situations and events that aren't anything to be afraid of. When we're young, the people around us are supposed to help us understand the difference between what's real and what's not real. They gently and persistently remind us that it's not okay to talk to strangers. They also get down on the floor with us and look under the bed to prove that there aren't any monsters there.

Fear can be tricky too. When we're growing up, we might be afraid to ask questions about things we're afraid of. No one wants to be perceived as being a "baby," and only babies get scared. Babies get laughed at too. Instead, we get scared, and end up staying scared until someone or something comes along and takes our mind off of being scared. The problem here is that the next time you find yourself in a similar situation, you're brain is still going to send you messages that there's a reason to be scared—even if there isn't.

The F.E.A.R. Factor

By now you've read enough about filters to wonder if there is a fear filter too. There isn't. It would be great if fear was an individual filter we could look at and work on, but it isn't.

Filters help us make decisions about what we see and think about the world around us. Fear isn't a conscious action. It's a reaction—a response. It isn't a conscious decision. It's not like we would stop and say to ourselves, "You know what... I think I'm going to be afraid here. Yes, I'm looking around and I think this situation calls for me to start shaking in my boots. So, in about two seconds, I'm going to do whatever I have to do to get myself out of this situation."

That's why our fear response is so important. It reacts quicker than we can think. Fear is our brains way of getting us to do whatever it is we have to do to stay safe. There's just a huge difference between a fear response designed to keep us alive, and a fear response that interferes with our ability to live our life.

Say there's someone you really want to meet or talk to, and that person is suddenly right in front of you. You're excited, but you might end up passing on the opportunity simply because your brain can't be sure that the other person is going to be receptive to talking with you. You contemplate how to handle the situation while your brain worries you might suffer an injury—in this case an emotional injury—so it starts waving a red danger flag and you step back deciding it might be safer to wait for a better opportunity. Suddenly, waiting feels like the right thing to do.

There's no real danger here other than maybe being embarrassed if things don't go the way you had hoped. Your brain doesn't see it that way though. It cares just as much about the emotional harm you might suffer as it does any physical harm. It just wants you to be safe. Because it operates in the background of your mind outside of your thoughts, you don't pay too much attention to it. You definitely hear its messages though – "Don't!" "Stop!" "Wait!"

Fear doesn't need its own filter. Instead, it sits in the background monitoring all of our filters with the singular goal of influencing our behavior in ways that will keep us safe.

There's a great acronym for fear: **FEAR** = **F**alse **E**vidence **A**ppearing **R**eal. While real fears—fears based on physical danger—serve to keep us safe, false fears try to get us to avoid the unknown.

Think about your role model filter for example. Has there ever been a time when you wanted to approach someone you thought the world of, but you never did? Why not? No doubt your reasons felt real enough at the time, but I'm willing to bet that if you wrote those reasons down on paper now, each one could be traced back to some piece of *False Evidence Appearing Real*.

The most annoying thing about this kind of fear is that it hides really well. A majority of the time we don't even realize we're being influenced by it. We just look around, get nervous for no apparent reason, and then move in a different direction because it feels like it's the right thing to do—the better, safer, or easier thing to do.

Our minds are also capable of taking a tiny particle of evidence and blowing it up into something totally out of proportion with reality. Phobias are good examples of that. Yes, it's legitimate to be afraid of the snake you see in the middle of the path while you're hiking. It's probably not a good thing if you're having the same response when you see a snake on TV.

Over time, fears that go unnoticed, unrecognized, or unexamined can morph into great big generalized stockpiles of emotional and personal FEARs that have just as much

68

influence over us as our legitimate primal fears do.

When that happens, those FEARs are influencing the way we look through every one of our filters, convincing us that we should always take the safer path, the one with the least amount of risk. Each time we let our fears decide our actions though, they become more influential. They become the defense mechanisms we fall back on. And then, instead of saving our life, our fears start robbing us of our life.

Regrets Suck!

You don't have to be 90 years old to have regrets. We all know what it's like to wish we had said or done something instead of saying or doing nothing, or vice versa. That feeling has nothing to do with age. It's just that when we're younger, it's easier to dismiss the things we did or didn't do because there's still a lifetime of opportunity stretched out in front of us.

It seems so innocent too. After all, there's nothing wrong with deciding to wait for the perfect moment to approach a crush—is there? All we have to do is build up our confidence, and then just do it. But unresolved youthful FEARs evolve into unresolved adult-size FEARs that will continue to gain momentum and influence over us until we shine a light on them. Until then, the perfect moment remains elusive and we will continue to struggle with our self-confidence. How many chances and opportunities do you think will come and go over the next five years if your decisions are based solely on avoiding change and not taking any risks? How about the next ten?

We may have grown and matured beyond simple fears

like being afraid to fall asleep in a dark, but it's tough to outgrow fears we don't even realize we have. One of President Franklin Roosevelt's most famous quotes is: *"The only thing we have to fear is fear itself."* It's a tremendous statement that holds true for everyone.

And here's the thing... giving into our fears doesn't prevent failure or loss. In fact, it can cause it. When our fears get the better of us, we don't move forward. We don't take chances or risks. Instead, we sit and watch the people around us accomplish things and wonder how come they can do it when we can't. In reality though, people who succeed also fail. They have the same fears we have—the fear of failing, of not belonging, of not being successful, and of feeling like they just don't fit in.

One of the things that separates people who feel fear and still get things done from people who struggle to do something other than react is their ability to make the distinction between false fears and legitimate fears that require immediate attention. They don't take their success or failure for granted either. They just know they can choose to step beyond their FEARs.

A Seriously Big Question

They've also learned that they can dismiss many of the fears quietly trying to influence their decisions about taking risks by asking themselves one simple question. "What's the worst that can happen if I fail?" (Please note that it says *if I fail*, not *if I try*.) Now think back to your list of role models and the people you admire. It's hard to imagine that any of them made it to where they are without having to get past a few of their own epic failures. Everyone fails—everyone.

Bill Gates failed with the first product he tried to bring to market. The reason Steven King is so successful is because after receiving 30 rejections for his first novel, *Carrie*, and throwing it into the trash, his wife pulled it out and convinced him not to give up. Walt Disney was fired because he "lacked imagination." We all know the story of how many times Thomas Edison failed before he succeeded with creating the first light bulb. Michael Jordan was cut from his high school basketball team. Lady Gaga was let go by her first record label because they didn't like her music.

It would be easy to look at that list of people and think that they were more courageous than we could ever be, but that's not true. Everybody has FEAR in their life—including everybody on that list. Remember, they were all little kids once too. Some of them were probably afraid of the dark. They were teenagers, which means they were probably self-conscious and afraid of looking stupid, or dumb, or like a loser. They probably had parents, relatives, guidance counselors, and friends telling them what they should do too.

People who've experienced success understand the value of acknowledging their fears. Fears provide us with opportunities. If it weren't for fear, how would we ever know we had accomplished something? If there's no risk, then there's probably no reward either. The only real false evidence we need to get past is the idea that the safety and security of doing nothing will feel at least as good as success feels. That's just not true. The only thing anyone feels when they let their choices be guided by false evidence is regret.

Fear is an invitation to grow and change. It's evidence that you might be stuck in a rut or so entrenched in your comfort zone that you didn't even realize you were developing the

FEAR of trying anything different.

The existence of fear is evidence that we have hopes and dreams. If we didn't secretly want something more or better, there'd be nothing to fear.

Flexing Your Filters:

Are there fears that have been holding you back from trying to move towards a better life? If you're human, then the answer to that question is a resounding Yes! Make a list of five things you'd really like to have happen, but that you've been too afraid to reach for.

1. _____
_____
_____

2. _____
_____
_____

3. _____
_____
_____

4. _____
_____
_____

5. _____
_____
_____

For each item on your list, write down what the worst case scenario would be if you failed, and try to identify the scariest part of failing.

1. _____

_____

_____

_____

_____

2. _____

_____

_____

_____

_____

3. _____

_____

_____

_____

_____

4. _____

_____

_____

_____

_____

5. _____

_____

_____

_____

_____

Lastly, pick one of the things you identified as something you haven't reached for yet, and think about how it could be broken down into a series of smaller steps that aren't as scary.

Creating a list like this can help you identify your fears so you can decide if they're real—or not. When they're not, when they're actually FEARs, (which happens more than you think) you'll be in a position to make a plan free of old and outdated fears that have been holding you back.

7

How Fear Impacts Our Choices

There are a lot of people who believe that the best way to deal with fear is to just do whatever you're afraid of doing anyway. But that can be dangerous. There are things we should truly be afraid of. But before we can figure out if a fear is real or false, we have to acknowledge that it's there.

Take the fear of change as an example. Change probably terrifies more people than spiders. As evidence, look at all the people around you living lives they aren't happy with. On paper, making a few small changes would likely change their lives for the better, whether it's going back to school, ending an unhappy relationship, or simply trying something new.

While the solution to these people's unhappiness is seemingly simple, the reality is that many people continue to spend their days suffering rather than face the uncertainty of change. There's even an expression that encapsulates this condition: *Better the devil you know than the one you don't.*

All too often, people live that expression to its fullest. Even when they're miserable, they take refuge in the idea that they're safe right where they are. It's familiar, oddly comfortable, and they know they can survive because they're already living there and surviving.

It's normal for people to feel frightened of change, especially if that change carries some risk. Here's an example:

Your parents have told you that because you're good at math, you should consider a career in finance or business. Their motives are pure—they want you to have a career that can allow you to have a comfortable lifestyle and to be able to support a family.

Now you have a problem. You love your parents and you want to make them happy, but you aren't interested in business. You want to pursue a career in journalism—a job that doesn't pay nearly as much, but one that you have a passion for. You're afraid to talk to them and tell them you want something different than what they want for you because they might:

- Refuse to help you pay for school
- Tell you that you're making a big mistake
- Tell you that you aren't smart enough or wise enough, or that you don't have enough experience to make a decision like this on your own
- Remind you that they know better because they're older and wiser
- Tell you that you're going to fail if you don't follow their advice

You're in a tough spot now. You haven't even told them and yet all these fears about what they might say or do have you doubting yourself. But that's how false evidence works. It keeps you so focused on everything that could go wrong, that there's no room to consider what might go right. It's quite possible that you could talk to your parents and tell them you've decided you'd like to pursue journalism instead of business and they might:

- Be surprised

- Ask you a lot of questions about why you decided on journalism
- Ask you why you think journalism is better than business
- Tell you that they're impressed that you know what you want to do so early on
- Start remembering people they know who are journalists
- Be supportive of you and your education even if it is in a different field

So many people waste their lives focusing on what might go wrong. They look into the future and all they see are possible pitfalls and failures. When they do that, they become blind to a world full of opportunity—because nothing great happens without some type of risk. They look at those risks and think there's too much danger. Other people look at the exact same situation and think of it as an adventure.

Doing something like taking the risk and speaking up for yourself isn't a guarantee your parents are going to be happy with your decision, but not taking the risk and going along with what someone else says simply because you fear what *might* happen is a guaranteed failure. It's like sitting on the sidelines and expecting to win the game from there—not going to happen. If you want any chance of scoring, you have to get up and play.

The Mind Is a Powerful Tool

The mind is truly an extraordinary thing. It can be our greatest asset as well as our greatest weakness, and it's amazing how many battles are waged between our ears without us even realizing it. It's the field of battle where our fears and doubts take on our hopes and dreams. And even though it's all taking place in our imagination, it can feel as real as anything else in our lives.

But now you know different. Now you know that when you feel fear, and you're sure you're physically safe (in other words, there aren't any dinosaurs trying to eat you), chances are very good that the fear you're feeling is nothing more than false evidence trying to appear real so it can take control of how you look at the world—no matter which filter you're looking through.

Now that you know this, you have a choice. You can continue to let FEAR be the defense mechanism that gives you permission to always take the safe route. You can continue to tell yourself that you're not ready, or that you're too busy, or that whatever it is you've been thinking about trying just isn't meant for you.

Or, you can start paying attention to the FEARs that are doing nothing more than holding you back from living and experiencing a life that's rewarding and truly yours. Yes, you might fail, but failing is rarely dangerous to your health or well being. What is dangerous is being trapped in a life you don't know how to escape.

No Time Like the Present

It's hard to imagine that a simple fear could evolve into a life-altering struggle, but it can. For some people, the fears they live with every second of every day become so strong that it causes them physical, mental, and emotional pain. They don't know how to escape, so they simply keep swallowing their stress or unhappiness, trying to deny that it exists because they can't bear the thought that it will never go away.

Sadly, there are drugs and alcohol as well as other destructive behaviors to turn to as momentary escapes from unhappy and unfulfilling lives. The evidence that's real here is the reality that regardless of the means of escape, the longer someone waits to acknowledge and face their fears, the stronger they become, and the harder it will be to deal with them.

The Process

Imagine you're standing in front of your closet. You've decided it's time to weed through your clothes, so you take each shirt, pair of pants, coat, etc. out of the closet, one by one, and look at it. Examining each piece of clothing on its own makes it easy to divide things into 3 piles—the keeper pile, the maybe pile, and the absolute NO! pile.

Examining your fears is a bit like that. There are going to be fears that you instinctively and immediately know are good to have around. The healthy fear that has you looking both ways before you cross the road is a keeper. You don't even have to think about whether the evidence that supports it is real or not; and there are lots of fears that are like that. They aren't exactly what you would call primal, but they definitely provide a healthy aversion to things and activities that might hurt, harm, or kill you.

The same goes for the other end of the spectrum. Everybody has silly little fears they didn't even realize they had until they started looking around. For example, lots of people have a fear of clowns. I can understand that. Clowns can be downright creepy sometimes. But if you're a guy, and that fear of clowns somehow gets generalized into a fear of women who wear a lot of makeup because there might be a serial killer lurking underneath, well, just exposing that one to the light of day is probably all it will take to put it in its proper perspective.

As you can tell, it's not too hard to determine which fears are keepers and which ones go into the NO! pile. It's the ones in between that are a challenge.

The To Be or Not to Be Conundrum

One of the reasons a fear ends up sticking around is because we haven't really made a decision about it. Say someone is bullying you. The filter that helps you understand what's going on is doing a great job of reminding you that it's the bully who has the real problem. And that's good, but your immediate problem is that the bully has chosen you as his or her current target.

The reason this is a problem for you is because you already know a bunch of good ways to deal with this problem. You can talk to someone about it. You can ask someone for help. You can stand up and face the bully yourself. Etc. They all sound easy enough, but for some reason, you just can't seem to do any of them.

But maybe your fear isn't really about what the bully is saying or doing. Maybe the fear is that you're afraid that if you bring it to more people's attention, they'll believe the bully is right about you, and think less of you as a result. It would be like when a bully steals someone's shoes. If the person doesn't bring it to anyone's attention, maybe no one will notice.

And that's how people get stuck behind false evidence that appears real. They want to do something, but they don't want everybody to know about their problem. They believe that not doing anything to change the situation will limit the number of people that will look at them and say or think, "Wow, you are truly weird."

The FEAR of being exposed provides a whole basket of solutions: hide, bury the problem, ignore the situation, pretend it isn't happening, suck it up, blame it on someone else, etc. None of these actions will solve the problem, but they can provide a temporary escape, and possibly even limit the amount of damage you experience.

That's why it's so easy to get stuck. It's tough to decide whether to be the person who stands up, or to be the person who doesn't make a fuss. But here's the thing; we've pretty much established what happens when you don't do anything—nothing good. It's better to make a choice than it is to be like Tarzan, suspended between two trees, holding onto to both vines, because you're not sure which one will take you in the right direction. As long as you're stuck between those two decisions, you aren't going anywhere, and sooner or later you're going to start feeling like you're being torn apart.

If You Choose Not to Decide, You Still Have Made a Choice

The questions you can ask yourself when you find yourself in situations like this are straight forward. "If it's all going to fall apart anyway, if I'm going to fail, what would I rather be doing when it happens. Would I rather go down trying to fix the problem? Or would I rather go down trying to escape the problem?"

Remember that fears thrive on worst case scenario thinking. Also remember that the worst failure only happens when you do nothing. It doesn't take courage to act under tough circumstances. It comes down to choosing which side you'd rather be on when it's all said and done—even if things didn't work out the way you'd hoped.

You've probably heard of a "Hail Mary" pass in football. It's the pass that the losing team makes during the last play of the game. If the pass is caught, they win the game. If the pass isn't completed, they lose. The team making the pass was going to lose the game anyway. They could have just resigned themselves to losing, but they didn't. They chose to pursue success right to the end. They understood that sometimes failure and success follow the same path. The only way to know which path you're on is to decide which one it is.

No one—absolutely no one—can ever take that choice away from you.

Flexing Your Filters:

With this exercise, it's time to celebrate the success you've had with overcoming your fears. I know it's hard to believe that we've overcome any fears sometimes, but we all have. And if we can do it once, then we can do it again. And every time we overcome one fear, we have both evidence that it can be done, and evidence that we can do it.

List ten fears you've overcome since you were a kid, along with how you overcame them.

1. _____

_____

_____

2. _____

_____

_____

3. _____

_____

_____

4. _____

_____

_____

5. _____

_____

_____

6. _____
_____

7. _____
_____

8. _____
_____

9. _____
_____

10. _____
_____

Celebrate overcoming your fears... even the small ones. It will build your confidence and make choices both clearer and less scary. The more we do anything in life the better we get at it. This is one of those exercises that you can and should do every few months. The more often you do it, the more evidence you'll have that you can identify *False Evidence Appearing Real* so you can keep making choices that support you moving in a good direction.

8

Choices

Now that you're beginning to grasp the ways your fears can covertly influence how you think and act, it will get easier and easier to recognize when it's happening. With a little practice, you won't be as likely to react out of habit. Instead, you'll realize that when your awareness isn't clouded by fear, you start becoming aware of opportunities for making better choices that will lead to better results with fewer regrets.

I'm going to let you in on a secret. Most people learn about the consequences of choices the hard way because no one ever taught them how to make a choice. It seems like it would be a no-brainer to figure it out, but when you're young, you aren't always given enough choices to develop a strong choice muscle. Choosing between chocolate or vanilla is hardly good preparation for choosing whether or not to accept the beer a friend is trying to hand you when you're 16 years old.

In school, you might be able to make a choice about which book to read in English class, but you aren't likely to be given a choice about how you'll be expected to prove that you've read it. Schools don't give you choices about which rules you can follow or ignore. But neither do your parents or society.

In fact, making choices can be downright difficult if you haven't had the opportunity to "practice" being in control of your life. What do I mean by "practice?" Up to this point in your life, the major choices and decisions about where you lived, who you lived with, and how you occupied your time have most likely been made by your parents or guardians. We need that structure when we're young to be safe, but sooner or later we're going to reach a point in time when we'll be expected to start making choices on our own. And no, it isn't fair for the people around us to just assume that we've somehow magically figured out how to make a good choice, or to fully comprehend all the choices that are available to us.

Choice 101

The next time you go to school or your job, look around and see if you can figure out which people look like they're making their own choices. It's pretty easy to spot them. They're very often leaders. They aren't following other people around, and they boldly walk in directions of their own choosing. Their confidence can be downright compelling.

It's just as easy to pick out the people who still might not have figured out that they can make their own choices. They are people content to follow others, or to sit on the sidelines unsure of what else to do. Not that there's anything wrong with either of these two situations. It's just disheartening to think that the reason someone hasn't started pursuing things they might enjoy is because their lives have been so filled with people making decisions for them that they didn't realize they even had a choice.

Another reason some people are slow to take on the challenge of developing their choice-making muscle is quite simply because it can be scary to think about what might happen if they make the wrong choice. So, instead of choosing, they let things play out hoping everything will turn out okay.

The reality is that not making a choice is actually a choice. It's just a choice to do nothing... and that's a choice whose roots are solidly planted in our fears. It might be the fear of not making the right choice, or of making the wrong choice, or of everything falling apart as a result of our choice. Would it make things easier if I pointed out the fact that everyone starts in this same place—the place where each of us makes that first conscious choice, the one that means we're starting to take hold of the reins of our own life?

It's too bad we aren't taught about choice when we're in school. If we were, it might not feel so overwhelming to realize that we're already making choices all day long. Even now, as I'm writing this, I'm trying to talk about choice in a way that won't be too overwhelming to contemplate. But maybe it's just better to get it all out in the open so we can get to all the good parts of choice.

Choices and Consequences

Even when we aren't aware of it, we spend our days making choices. Everything we say and do is the result of a choice. The trick is raising our awareness. Take brushing your teeth for example. Once you make the choice to brush your teeth on a daily basis, you don't have to make that choice every day. The first conscious choice to brush is enough to set the habit in motion.

It's the same for other choices too—like when we decide to give up eating meat, or not to smoke, or to be nice to someone. These are each choices that may have taken some thought and consideration at first, but once we got our thoughts in order, we were ready to make our choice.

But this is the same reason why it's so easy to grow up without making any real choices. If someone is always there to tell you should brush your teeth every day, even if you do it for the rest of your life, might it be because someone else installed the habit for you rather than because *you* made the choice to do it? If you were raised in a vegetarian household, how would you know if the reason you don't eat meat is because of a choice you consciously made, or the result of a vegetarian habit that developed from being raised in a vegetarian home? There's nothing to say that you wouldn't have become a vegetarian on your own. It's just a question of whether you've ever put any of your own thought into affirming the choice.

The people who make choices for us when we're young generally have the best of intentions, but it can and will limit our future ability to make a choice, especially when it comes to the serious choices we face, like when we're being pressured by our peers. On the other hand, if we've been taught from an early age that every action we take is the result of a choice we've made, we already understand how much more exciting it is to be more involved in our own life. Yes, it can be stressful when we're faced with a choice, but it's exciting to make those first choices too.

Too many people only put care and thought into their choices later in life when most of the major decisions they should've been involved with are already behind them. These people—like too many others—have left too much of their lives up to other people's choices. These are the same people who use blame and excuses so they can feel better about themselves, and about not living the lives they could have chosen years before.

Fortunately, it's never too late to start exercising your choice muscle. The sooner you start, the less likely you are to be overwhelmed by the choices that life is going to toss your way. In fact, there's a reason why the chapter on fear preceded this one. Every one of our initial conscious choices has an element of FEAR (false evidence appearing real) neatly buried beneath the surface warning us against making any choices outside of our normal comfort zone. "What makes you think you can do this?" and "Why would you want to do that?" are typical questions FEAR might use to get us to avoid making a choice. After all, if someone else makes the choice for us and it all falls apart, then there's someone else handy to take all the blame.

If the prospect of being in charge of your own choices is still frightening, then consider these two realities. The first is that you can't ever really be sure of the thought process someone else is using when they're making their choices. It's all well and good to believe that someone else has done a good job of considering all the possibilities, or has your best interest at heart, but that doesn't make it so. People always have their own reasons for doing things, and sadly, history is full of evidence of inspiring and compelling people with hidden agendas making choices for entire races and/or countries with horrendous consequences.

The second is that even if you struggle with making choices, or are fearful of making choices because you don't feel confident enough to make the "right" choice, you're still making choices that will affect you future. There's always the risk of making the "wrong" choice, but which would you rather deal with at the end of the day? Not making a choice and never knowing if you could have actually accomplished something? Or having made the choice, failed, and learned what not to do next time? And who knows, you might have made a choice that worked out exactly the way you'd hoped!

Regret is one of the results of not taking charge and exercising your choice muscle. A lifetime of regret is the result of never grasping the truth that FEAR can't actually stop anyone from doing anything.

Choices Open Up a World of Possibilities

Regret is a burden too many people live with. Some regret never chasing a dream or having accepted the abusive behavior that has permeated their entire life. Some simply regret not following a path that's true to who they are on the inside.

Whatever the source of their regret, at some point, each of those individuals has stopped and asked themselves, "How did I get here?" The answer is that they got there through a series of choices. But it's one thing to be 20 years old and asking this question when you have decades of opportunity stretching out ahead of you. It's quite another to be asking it when you're 60 years old, an age that you should have every expectation of reaching. How old will you be when you ask yourself, "How did I get here?" for the first time?

Every day, we have choices to make. Even when those choices seem relatively inconsequential, the reality is that combined, they're all leading us somewhere. Wouldn't it be better to have those choices guided by our true dreams and desires?

Take a look at your role models. Isn't that how they've lived their lives? Making choices they believed would lead them to their dreams? They didn't get where they are now because they were lucky. They worked at it. They made everyday choices they trusted would keep them moving in the right direction.

And please don't make the mistake of thinking that successful people must not be as afraid as you might be. Remember, FEAR can't actually stop anyone from doing something they are committed to doing. In most cases, FEAR is nothing more than an illusion designed to keep you from stretching beyond the safety of your comfort zone. Once you start making choices, you can deliberately look for the FEAR and decide for yourself if it's real, or nothing worth paying any attention to.

The Balloon and the Anchor

As soon as you accept that you've been making choices all along, a look at your life is going to reveal the results of those choices. The evidence is all there in your circle of friends, the way you spend your time, the way you feel about your life, etc. Jim Rohn also said that we are the average of the five people we spend the most time with. Who are those people for you? If the answer makes you wince, it might be a good idea to become more proactive about who those five people are. That's not to say you should dismiss people you've known and loved forever. It is suggesting that they might not be the best people to advice you when it comes to making choices.

The people we allow into our lives are either balloons or anchors; they either raise us up or weigh us down. The "anchors" are very often people who ignore our insecurities while simultaneously filling a void in our life. They provide us with the comfort of knowing that they aren't likely to challenge us, expect more out of us, or urge us on to be more than we are. In return, we do the same for them.

Anchors don't want us to grow or change because then we might expect them to grow or change too. Nor are they likely to solve any of our problems. Sadly, their status as anchors isn't likely to change either—unless you and your fellow anchors decide together that you're ready to proactively make better and more conscious choices.

"Balloon" people are people who have a genuine interest in seeing us succeed. They are the people who complement our personalities in a good way. They don't proclaim that they can fix us. They really care about us and understand that our life is our life.

Choosing our companions can be one of the most profound choices any of us makes. The people we choose as friends say a lot about who we are and how we treat people. If someone has nice friends, it's easy to think that he or she is likely to be nice too. If your social circle includes friends and acquaintances that fall into the balloon category of people who are respectful, trustworthy, and likable, the people who meet you are more likely to perceive you as being the same. At the very least, you aren't likely to be embarrassed to introduce or be seen with them.

Other Balloons and Anchors

We also have a tendency to look at the choices we're facing and quickly categorize them as good or bad choices— aka balloons or anchors. For example, at some point we all have to think about getting a job, or working, or finding a way to support ourselves. Look at people who've already made their job choice and it's easy to see how this choice could be thought of as an anchor choice.

How many people do you know who are truly happy with what they're doing? People moan about their jobs so much that it's a wonder anyone looks forward to getting up in the morning and joining the thousands of other people who aren't looking forward to going to work either. They work all day, go home, go online, go to sleep, and then get up the next morning to do it all over again.

When you see people doing that day after day, it's very easy to speculate that no matter what job you pick, it's going to end up being an anchor. And to be truthful, it happens. But one of the biggest reasons it happens is because our FEARs about things like money, necessity, responsibilities, public opinion about what we should do with our lives, our lack of education to pursue something better, etc., end up overwhelming our dreams and desires of doing something we truly believe would make us happy.

This is not to say that anyone should disregard common sense when it comes to making those kinds of choices. But there's a difference between addressing your FEARs with a decision that's going to stretch your comfort zone, and deciding to sit in a room and play video games sixteen hours a day because that's what you love to do the most. If you really love video games, there's got to be a career track that could get you into the industry where your "balloon" job exists.

Making Better Choices

It doesn't matter if you use the balloon/anchor analogy with people, jobs, careers, or your down time. All anchors are composed of fear, and they will continue to interfere with your ability to make better choices for better reasons as long as you continue to avoid looking at them long enough to figure out if they're real, or simply FEAR—more false evidence appearing real. Truly, most of them disappear when they are exposed to the light of day.

And remember, you want your choices to be a reflection of the filters you've been building. That's where your decisions about who you are and who you want to be reside. You've been getting to know what's in your filters throughout the course of this book, but up until now, it might have been more practice than theory. Right now, your filters are the balloons, and your FEARs are the anchors keeping those balloons from growing, stretching, and reaching new heights.

Making choices gets easier with practice too. Don't decide to exercise your choice muscles for the first time by starting with a complex or tough choice. Start with something simple like why you hate one of your classes so much. If you hate it, I can almost guarantee there's a fear of something buried in there somewhere.

For example, maybe what you really hate about your history class is that the teacher uses too many true/false questions on tests and quizzes, and for some reason you always seem to get them wrong. Now your history grade is slipping as a result, and you hate that! Like I said, fear likes to hide. If this person was you, and you didn't sit down long enough to look below the surface and figure out what was really bothering you, you might not ever realize that it didn't have anything to do with history. You could even end up going through your entire life hating everything about history. And that would have been a true waste of your energy.

There's so much potential in understanding this truth.

Each of us has the ability to face our FEARs, and we aren't doing ourselves any favors by putting it off. We can't escape the fact that our lives are filled with choices. But when we understand what choice is really about—being able to consider our options without letting the fear of what could go wrong take over—we make better choices.

The real trick is not to try and do it as an all-at-once kind of activity. When trying to expose any kind of fear, the best approach is slow and steady. Over time, you'll get better and faster at it. Each time an underlying FEAR is exposed and addressed, its power to covertly influence your future choices and decisions is diminished. That's when the choices you face can become really exciting, because with each diminished fear, the qualities of your filters begin to shine and your confidence in your ability to make good choices grows.

Yes, there will be tough choices to make throughout your life, and not every choice is going to work out the way you had hoped, but that's a situation everyone else is in too. The biggest difference for people who take charge of their choices is that even when they fail, they know they reached for something all the same. They didn't let FEAR hold them back.

Don't let your fears—both real and imagined—become anchors that hold you back. Don't let FEAR convince you that people can't ever really be happy. In fact, being happy begins with a choice. Most people just don't realize how the FEAR residing in them is interfering.

There's a saying, "Nobody ever lays on their deathbed and wishes they'd spent another day at the office." When you embrace the potential of what taking charge of your own choices can achieve, you won't have to worry about feeling that way at any point in your life.

Flexing Your Filters:

As was said earlier, understanding what choices are really all about begins with realizing that we are always making choices. For example, maybe you decided you were going to do your homework before dinner, or, you decided to put it off until later. Either way, the choice about when it gets done is totally yours. So let's start with you writing down three things you did over the past few days that were truly the result of your own choices.

1. _____

2. _____

3. _____

Look back over the past few days and come up with three times when you did something because of someone else's choice(s). For example, maybe a group of people were talking about something you didn't really want to talk about, but you ended up adding something to the conversation anyway.

1. _____

2. _____

3. _____

Each of those situations is an example of how easy it is to end up accepting and going along with someone else's choices. For each one of the choices you just listed, can you identify why you went along with someone else's choice? I'm not going to suggest there is a FEAR buried in each example. I am going to ask you to be honest with yourself about looking for one though. It's not to make you feel bad. It's so you can start seeing things that might be influencing you more than you were aware of.

1. _____

2. _____

3. _____

_____

Take a couple of minutes to be proud of yourself here too. You've earned it. It's not easy looking for things we'd rather not find. But it is empowering. It's proof that no matter what anyone else says or does, you can make choices for yourself. All you have to do is start small and work your way up to tackling the challenge of tougher choices.

P.S. Lastly, I can't let this chapter go by without bringing up situations when it looks like we don't have any choice or chance at all. Sadly, there are times when our choices don't stand a chance in the physical world. Victims don't choose to be victims. Prisoners of war don't choose to be prisoners of war. Etc. There's a tremendous amount of real fear that comes into play in those situations because there's very often no choice for the person to make that will change what's happening.

What I can say is that even when someone can't change what's going on around them, they can still make choices about what's going on within them. Regardless of what we are subjected to, we get to make the choice about who _we_ are, and no one can ever take that away from us. Granted, there are times when the help of a professional might be needed, but even that will never change the fact that we have the right to choose.

9

Experiences

Now it's time to talk about our experiences. In the last chapter we talked about choices, and how the things we do are actually the result of a choice we've made whether we're aware of it or not. But if that's the case, how are we supposed to make a choice when the only experience we have to base our future choices on is in our past? How can we make choices if we don't have enough good or positive experiences from the past to build on?

The first thing to do is to give ourselves time to learn how to use our experiences to our best advantage. This is another one of those things no one really teaches us about. And if no one explains it to you, it can be a long time before you encounter a point in your life where you say, "Enough! It's time to change things up."

It isn't always the result of one dramatic experience either. It can start with small things like simply saying to yourself that you've had enough of your room looking like its suffered through an apocalyptic event. It can be when you decide you've had enough of getting grades lower than you know you're capable of achieving. Or when you decide you've experienced enough peer pressure from people who clearly don't care about you anyway. But it can also happen in an instant with a big bang experience—like when the person you love hits you, cheats on you, or betrays your trust.

There is no one single defining moment or threshold to cross. In fact, it can happen as a result of reading these words right here, right now. All that matters is that you recognize this experience for what it is—an opportunity to start making choices that support who you are, and who you want to be. This is when our past, both the good and the bad, come into play.

Did you know that when we think about our past we aren't recalling the actual event (unless you have an eidetic memory)? We're recalling the parts of our past that had the most impact on us at the time. This is good because it means all the stuff that didn't impact us as strongly isn't likely to be something we have to think about. But the really great thing about this is that it makes it much easier to identify what we definitely didn't like. If we can identify those parts of our experiences, then we know we can start thinking about ways to prevent them from happening again. We can do the same thing with good memories from our past too. We can look at them and start thinking about what we can do to increase the likelihood that they'll happen again.

Some people will call this "learning the lessons taught by our past." But if that was all it took to make a better choice, most people wouldn't make the same mistake twice. There'd be less drug and alcohol abuse, and fewer teens dropping out of school and ending up in jail. Recognizing a lesson isn't enough. If we don't want our future filled with the same types of experiences as we've had in our past, we first need to figure out what we do and don't have absolute control over.

For example, if a child grows up with an abusive alcoholic parent, there's very little that child could have done to stop or prevent what happened. They were just a child. They didn't have the knowledge or the power to make the choices that could have stopped or changed what a full grown adult was going to do. For any change to take place, it would have to have been the result of the adult making a choice.

We could look at a situation like that and see it as black or white, but living through a situation like that doesn't automatically make a child bad or good. Ultimately though, that child could grow up and continue to boil down their experience until only blaming and excuses are left. You might even know someone like this, the person who continually repeats to themselves and the world, "I am who I am because of what's happened to me."

I don't like phrases like "turning points" or "the moment of truth" because they are really cliché. But when a child is growing up, there's every chance that they're going to experience one of those life changing moments when they realize that what happened to them wasn't their fault, and that they didn't have the power to change what they experienced growing up. They might even start to consider the idea that there's nothing wrong with them.

This is such a powerful thought. Sadly, many young people experience that first moment of hope and relief and don't know what to do next. It's like they've been a hostage for so long they don't know how to deal with a thought that's so different from their normal thoughts. The memory of that hopeful moment doesn't disappear though. Instead, it gets stuck in a kind of limbo waiting until something else comes along to give it another nudge. Each nudge adds to the last, building momentum towards the moment when they actually start thinking about making their own choices as a way of changing their experience.

This can be a challenging moment too because it exposes

the truth that everyone gets to make their own choices, including all the people in our lives who've been so wrapped up in their own dramas that they didn't see or care about the situations the children around them were experiencing as a result. But what a relief it is to figure this out! It's not within one person's power to fix another person's choices. It's not one person's job to fix another person's choices. Even when it's for all the right reasons, it's not going to work. People make their own choices for their own reasons.

But this is also another point where people can get stuck because they might be too embarrassed or ashamed about their past to even conceive of asking for someone's help or support with figuring out what to do next. Fortunately, with the internet, people who feel too trapped to reach out where they live can find valuable information, ideas, and wisdom to help them start making better choices for themselves.

It's an exciting time for us when we're ready to stop letting ourselves be defined by our past choices and experiences. It can be challenging when we've been making the same choices for a long time, but comforting to know that we can start taking control of our choices to create our future experiences. The past is the past, and our past experiences can't harm us anymore. We're still going to encounter situations that bring up our past and threaten to interfere with our filters, but now we're able to recognize what's happening and see if for what it is—an opportunity to remember who we choose to be *now*.

Every Experience is a Lesson and an Opportunity

Our experiences don't just reside in our long ago past.

Every part of our day is comprised of experiences—some good, some bad, some more or less important than others. Because there are so many, it's easy to think that we only need to pay attention to those big profound life experiences that jump right out at us. Thinking like this leads to too many missed opportunities for making choices that are going to lead to experiences we're happy to have a memory of.

There's something very inspiring about knowing that you made a choice, and something worthwhile came out of it. And this can also be the case with situations that are emotionally challenging—like when you have to end a relationship, or have to go to a funeral. Neither of these is a happy time, but when you make your choices for meaningful reasons, you'll feel stronger and more purposeful with your actions.

Every day we are presented with the opportunity to think about how things went. Did we make good choices? Bad choices? Did we give into other people's choices? When we take the time to look at all the little choices we make throughout the day, we're going to notice how they add up. Over time, those choices become our habits, and our habits become the patterns we live our lives by.

Think of a choice as if it was a 16 ounce bottle of regular soda. Did you know that if you drink one soda a day for a year you'll have consumed over 19 pounds worth of calories? It's the same with the choices we make though. If we make the same choices day after day, they're going to add up. Yes, we can always wait for something to happen before we decide it's time to think about some of the choices we're making, but the longer we wait, the harder it is to deal with. Think about that bottle of soda again. Which is easier to do: make the choice to pass on the soda because you don't really want to drink that many pounds, or ignore the consequences of a soda-a-day habit until the end of the year when you have 19 pounds to lose?

The more you get used to the idea that you get to make choices, the easier it gets to make choices that lead to better experiences. You won't always get it right, but no one does. It's just important to understand that our choices become our habits, and our habits set us on a path towards our future.

I Screwed Up. Now What?

Learning from an experience doesn't have to be limited to how we learn from our epic failures. Unfortunately, many of us seem to need to experience a bigger failure before we start paying attention. For example: Mary applied for admission to the school of her dreams but didn't get accepted. It's a crushing experience for her because she'd planned to attend this school with her friends. It was also her parent's alma mater.

What can Mary do now? The college has said no, and it's not like she's feeling inspired to drive to the college and ask the admissions board why she was denied. And even if she did ask, she might not be able to get a direct answer from them. Right now, Mary feels awful, and who can blame her?

Sometimes the lessons being offered up by our experiences can really suck. Mary could take this experience and decide it's evidence that she's a failure who doesn't deserve to go the school. And yes, she may have failed at being accepted by her first pick, but a word like "failure" carries with it the implication that something about *her* is a failure.

People are too quick to label themselves as failures when they don't get the result they wanted, or too quick to accept their failures as confirmation of all the negative things they've been led to believe about themselves. But everybody has failed at something—usually many times over. The only true failure is in failing to make an effort, and that's the easiest failure of all to turn around. All it requires is another attempt. Anyone not willing to give something another try is using failure as an excuse.

Mary could switch over to denial and deliberately ignore all the questions and thoughts popping into her mind. "Why didn't I try harder to get better grades?" "I should have taken more time with the essay." "It's my own fault. I know I could have done better."

But denial is time wasted on avoiding the inevitable. If Mary could have gotten better grades and didn't, then the idea that it might actually be her own fault that she wasn't accepted is already circulating through her thoughts. She also instinctively knows if she spent enough time on her essay, or on activities that colleges like to see listed on applications.

Denial accomplishes nothing. Everyone is allowed to spend a little quality time with their distress, shame, and failures, but hopefully that time doesn't expand into a long-term pity-party where we start losing ground. Our failures are, after all, in the past. The less time wasted on denial, dwelling on what could have been, and/or self-pity, the sooner we're able to start thinking about choices that will have us moving in a better direction.

Granted, Mary's immediate situation might not be ideal, but it is a starting point. And that's what our experiences do for us—they give us a new starting point with the opportunity to take control of what we do next. Mary could decide to go to community college for a semester and then try to transfer. She could retake the SATs to improve her score. Or, if she's still a junior, she could increase the number of activities she participates in. If she isn't comfortable being a year behind her friends in college, she could seek out a different school. And who knows what possibilities those options might open up for her as a result of her new course of action?

With all that we know about Mary now, it would be easy for us to look back at her experience and wonder if she knew what was happening at the time. Did she know that her steady B average might not be good enough for college? Did she consider doing something else with her time other than being online? There's no way to say. The only thing we can say is that if she'd thought more about where her experiences were leading her, she might have been able to see that her current choices were brewing future problems.

At the very least, Mary's situation is evidence that even when our choices lead to experiences we don't enjoy, we have the opportunity to think twice before making the same choice again. Another thing we can take away from Mary's experience is that taking stock of what's going on now, can help us limit the number of unpleasant experiences we might unconsciously be heading towards in our future. No one can avoid everything, but it definitely feels better to know that you tried than it does to fail simply because you did nothing.

People really can change something about themselves or their life in an instant. It happens all the time. Chances are good that you've done it yourself. It's just that up until now, you've probably been making those choices without realizing what they mean in the long-term. You might have decided to give up soda, or to start seriously working out, or to study harder. You were able to do it because you recognized an experience that you didn't like, and figured out what choices might lead you to a future experience you would like.

Give Yourself a Chance

Too many of my childhood memories were of experiences I never wanted to experience again. I certainly didn't want to grow up, get married, and have my future children experience them. Like most people, I wanted to be happy, so when I started thinking about what I wanted to do with my life, I used my past experiences to help me decide.

I knew I liked people, psychology, and sociology, but, I wasn't entirely sure how I would apply those disciplines in a career setting. In high school, my experience was that there wasn't a supportive role model I felt like I could talk to. In this case, my negative experience helped me make the choice to become the person I'd needed when I was in high school. I wanted to be there for kids who didn't know where to turn, or who to turn to. I chose to be the guy who said, "I know what you're going through is tough, so let me help you." That was my choice, and I've never regretted it.

You'll also be able to use your experiences to help you make exciting decisions about your future. Obviously there are many questions to consider, but don't underestimate the power of what you've already learned. What is it about some of your experiences—past and present—that makes them stand out more than others? What negatives could you turn into positives for someone else? What do you wish had been there when you needed it?

Becoming Part of a Community

One of the great things about using the ups and downs of life as an educational tool for yourself is the opportunity to use the lessons you've learned to help others. So much of the pain people carry around with them is related to the people who were in their lives when they were young. We know so much more about how and why this happens though. We understand what it means to "break the cycle."

As you become an adult, you're going to find yourself in situations where you're going to be able to give advice and counsel people you come in contact with. It could be someone younger, a peer, or maybe even one of your own children. The last thing you're going to want to do is pass along a negative world view. Having clear filters and a system for processing your experiences will put you in good stead when those opportunities come up.

I'm always inspired by people who are true role models, people ready to help others overcome the same challenges and setbacks they experienced. They aren't just counselors either. They can be athletes, doctors, moms, musicians, etc., who know the value of hearing someone say or do something that makes you feel like a worthwhile human being deserving of respect and dignity. Once you feel the truth of that experience for yourself, you're going to enjoy opportunities to pass it along to others who will benefit too.

The inspiring thing about all the people who are ready to help us along our path is that they all started out just like the rest of us. They had to plot their own path to clarity too, and they did it facing the same kinds of choices you are facing right now.

Flexing Your Filters:

As I said before, the good thing about the past is that it's in the past. Good or bad, now it's just a collection of experiences that can be used as information to help us organize our future. We just have to get used to recognizing it as the valuable resource it is.

Remember that your choices turn into your habits, and your habits set you on a path towards your future. If you want to have more experiences worth remembering, don't wait for monumental experiences to grab your attention. Make a choice to think about your experiences at regular intervals, and you're more likely to stay on course.

This exercise is for looking back over one day. Taking a look at one day is a good place to start when you're making new choices that will pave the way for new experiences. It's always easier to tweak things in the beginning. As your new choices become habits, you might not have to spend so much time with them, but you'll still want to look at them regularly. If you don't, you won't notice the small things that could end up throwing you completely off course somewhere in the future. Remember the impact one innocent bottle of soda can have over time!

Take some time to think about your day, and write down five different things you experienced. It doesn't have to be a minute-by-minute accounting. It just needs to be a list of things you actually remember doing—or participating in— during your day.

Your Path to Clarity

1. _____
_____
_____
_____
_____
_____

2. _____
_____
_____
_____
_____
_____

3. _____
_____
_____
_____
_____
_____

4. _____
_____
_____
_____
_____
_____

5. _____
_____
_____
_____
_____
_____

After you've written your list down, consider each activity, answering these three questions:

1. Did this activity go as well as I had hoped it would?
2. Is there something I could have done to have had a better outcome, or to have made this experience more enjoyable?
3. If I keep doing this activity the same way for the next year, what is the long-term result likely to be?

10

Self-Esteem – How do You Like Me Now?

What is self-esteem? The short answer is that self-esteem is how we feel about ourselves. But as you know, it's not that simple. We don't always feel the same way about ourselves. We might feel really good about ourselves one minute, and then turn a corner and feel the exact opposite in the next. It can happen like that because our self-esteem can be influenced and impacted, in both helpful and harmful ways, by people and situations.

The only thing we can definitely say about self-esteem right now is that we all have it. Other than that, it's just a broad-brush term used to describe the internal feelings we have about our value and self-worth when we're interacting with the external world. If the result of our interaction is a good result, our self-esteem is usually in a good place. If the result is bad, our self-esteem can suffer.

Under the Influence

One reality is that sometimes our level of self-esteem has more influence over our choices than our intelligence and common sense. If someone offers you drugs, in that moment, all your previous decisions and commitments to saying "no" can get buried under the fear of being seen as a "goodie two-shoes." A moment ago your self-esteem was strong enough to know what decision you should make, but in the next, it wasn't.

Another truth about self-esteem is that no matter how old you are, how much life experience you have, or how strong your self-esteem is, there will always be people and situations in your life that can instantly kick it up or down a notch. I know that might be hard to believe, but trust me when I tell you that your parents will always have the power to make you feel like a little kid no matter how old you are. If your parents are loving and supportive, that might be a nice thing. If your parents aren't, well, that won't be as nice.

Our self-esteem reflects our feelings of self-worth and of how much value we believe we add to the world around us, but that can be impacted too. Like when the star of a high school basketball team comes face to face with an NBA pro. Their level of self-esteem for how good they are takes a hit when it comes face to face with "real" skill. That same high school player might meet a gold medal winner from a Special Olympics basketball team and suddenly experience a very different kind of hit to their self-esteem.

Each of these situations makes one thing clear. Our feelings of self-esteem can rise or fall as the **result** of an interaction with someone or something, and we don't have to be thinking about it for it to happen. It's not like we walk around feeling great or bad about ourselves and suddenly stop to think, "Wow, my self-esteem is really high today" or "Wow, my self-esteem is really low today."

Instead, we have an experience and our level of self-esteem adjusts according to its own quick—sometimes completely wrong—interpretation of what just happened. What makes hits to our self-esteem so tough to deal with is that we rarely have control over the situations and/or people involved. Something happens, and our self-esteem just reacts.

You're Not Broken

"Sticks and stones may break my bones, but words will never hurt me." We've already covered the fact that this is a lie. Broken bones and bruises can heal, but the damage other people's words inflict on us can become deeply rooted in our definitions of who we think we are.

We all know how this feels. I don't care how popular or spectacular someone is, everyone knows how it feels when something happens and we're left wondering about our worth as a human being. Sometimes those happenings are small and easy to let go, but sometimes they completely trash our self-esteem and it feels like nothing good will ever happen again.

As bad as it is when this happens, we can all take comfort in knowing that no one escapes these kinds of experiences. On a constant basis, every one of us encounters people and situations with the potential of impacting and/or influencing our self-esteem in both positive and negative ways.

Our Self-esteem is Always in Play

Even when we aren't paying attention, our self-esteem is always in the background reacting to what's going on around us. It's never just sitting on the bench waiting to be called in. For example, a friend looks at the new shirt you're wearing, and smiles adding a half-chuckle. You have no idea what that means. When you looked in the mirror that morning, you thought you looked really good. And you don't dare to ask because you're afraid of the answer.

So you find a mirror and check to see if your shirt is inside out or something else has happened, but you see the exact same person wearing the exact same shirt. Now your self-esteem is confused. Who's right—you or your friend? Did your friend just insult you? Was he or she jealous because you looked really good? Does this mean you don't know how to pick out clothes?

Once some aspect of what we "thought" we believed about ourselves is challenged, our self-esteem becomes like a squeaky wheel persistently searching for information it can use to better determine our place and value in the world. The reason it can be so wishy-washy is because it tends to accept the results of our interactions with people and situations as evidence of the truth about who we are. After all, there are so many of them and only one of us.

For someone with limited life experience, a situation like the one above might end with them throwing away everything they were wearing that day and deciding that they have lousy taste in clothes. Over time, similar feelings can start to build up. And it's not like there's a lack of people happy to step up and tell us exactly who we are and how we should feel about ourselves. Obviously some of those people do this in a positive way, but it's quite another when the words and deeds of others send someone spiraling down their self-esteem scale towards dark and scary feelings like self-hate and self-loathing.

Cliques

Cliques are all about self-esteem. If you're a jock, you

share similar feelings about yourself as the jocks you hang around with. You accept things about the others in your jock clique because they accept things about you. If you're an "It Girl" then your self-esteem is going to be similar to the self-esteem of your fellow "It Girls."

It's the same within all cliques—each member silently commits to support everyone else's self-esteem with words and behaviors that will create the desired self-esteem result. For example, when Kim Kardashian tries out a new style, her clique pals are much more likely to rave than they are to say anything negative, regardless of whether they really love it or hate it. As a whole, the clique might accept one or two contrary opinions, but after that, the contrary person would be booted. No one wants to be booted out of their clique.

We all want to feel like we belong. We want to feel like we bring something of value to the table too, even if that value is nothing more than accepting the role of the lowest person in the clique. It might not be someone's first choice, but that person still gets all the advantages of being a part of the group—including the anticipated boost to their self-image. If the price is starting at the bottom, then so be it. Seriously, would it really be so bad to be the worst quarterback in the NFL? It's still the NFL.

And yet even people who are members of the most desirable cliques imaginable can struggle with their self-esteem. Why? Because they are just as likely as anybody else to get tangled up with trying to figure out who they really are. It's hard to build a realistic self-image when the only things someone hears about themselves is how good or great they are. No one is perfect and good all the time. Everyone has their moments, and inside of each of us is the desire to believe that we belong and have something of value to contribute

119

even when we don't believe we are as good or great as other people think we are.

It's the exact same situation for someone whose self-esteem is low because they've been experiencing more negative results than they know how to handle. None of us is imperfect or bad all the time either; especially when we're growing up and more susceptible to other people's interpretations of our mistakes and efforts. Inside each of us is a slightly different aspect of the same desire—to believe there is something good, or possibly even of great value within us that we can contribute regardless of what other people think.

We're all in the same boat when it comes to self-esteem. Our self-esteem is always in play, and it doesn't matter if it's mostly good or mostly bad feedback. It can be just as damaging to accept all the good feedback and think that's the real us, as it can be to accept all the negative feedback and think that's the real us.

Stand Tall

You've probably heard the phrase, "We teach other people how to treat us." There is some truth in the statement, but there's room for misinterpretation too because we don't always have a choice about how other people treat us. No one actively sets out to encourage others to treat them with prejudice and hate, but there are people who will treat them that way all the same. It certainly isn't fair to expect someone who has no control over a situation to change what they can't change. And remember, this applies to people who are perceived as living the *good* life as much as it does to people living in tough situations. The one thing both those people have in common is that they need a way to build up their self-esteem to get to the point where they can make a change.

I've met many students struggling with self-esteem because of what they've been told about themselves. Unfortunately, I don't always get the opportunity to really talk to them about what's going on. Instead, I get a few minutes—sometimes just a few seconds. Sometimes the only thing I get to say to them is to walk with their shoulders back and their chin up.

I know that sounds too silly and simple to work, but I've seen it work time and time again. One moment I'll see someone who looks completely distressed or discouraged, walking with their head down and their books clutched against their chest like a shield. And then I'll see a glint of hope in their eyes as they walk away standing taller. Obviously it isn't just about standing taller (although standing taller will always make you feel better). Doing something like standing tall is a way of interrupting the pattern of negative thoughts trying to take over your mind.

The Squeaky Wheel

You've also heard people say: "The squeaky wheel gets the grease." The reason it gets the grease is because the squeak is so annoying it interferes with our ability to think about anything else. Sometimes, that's the way it is with how we feel about ourselves. Something happens, one or more of our filters is challenged, and now it's like a squeaky wheel playing the event over and over and over. And then something really weird happens. Instead of being able to make it stop, we start to see and hear anything that's similar.

Back to the clothing challenge mentioned earlier. Suppose you managed to muster up enough self-esteem to decide that the problem wasn't with the way you looked. It was with the shirt. The color wasn't right, so you go out and buy another shirt that's a better color. You feel better about this one and decide to wear it the next day. This time, a different friend gives you a weird look. Will you be able to convince yourself that it's the shirt's fault this time too? Probably not, and it's not like you're going to ask, even though the look could have been about anything. Nope... you tried, the weird look you got was the result of your effort, and that's that. Now you feel even more like you don't have any control over whether you look good or stupid.

That's the problem—control. We can't always control what happens. We can't control what other people do either. And yet it's the squeaky-wheel results of those kinds of situations that we end up focusing on. We think that if we had done or said the "right" thing, there wouldn't be a problem. And that's why everybody struggles with their self-esteem regardless of their status. We all wish we could do and say the right things and escape the pain, frustration, and embarrassment that might be lurking right around the corner.

Is There a Self-Esteem Filter?

It's more like every filter has a level of self-esteem. Your clothing challenge may have convinced you that you're a disaster when it comes to picking out clothes, but maybe you play a killer guitar and feel really good about yourself from that perspective. A very nice popular girl might feel really good about herself while she's in school, but cry herself to sleep after helping a drunk parent to bed for the third night in a row.

It would be a lot easier if self-esteem was a solid yes or no situation, but it isn't. It's flexible. Fortunately, there are ways we can nurture and strengthen our own self-esteem.

Always remember that just because someone says something is true, that doesn't mean it is. When we're young, we're taught to believe what our parents, elders, mentors, and teachers tell us. We aren't encouraged to question what they say either. Is it any wonder that when we find ourselves in a situation where we should be asking questions we don't have the courage or skill to do it?

The next time you find yourself in a situation where you feel like someone just expects you to accept what you're being told—especially if it makes you feel bad about yourself—don't. I'm not suggesting you should get in someone's face. I am suggesting that before you believe what someone else proclaims about you or your situation, make sure you give yourself some time and space to think it out for yourself. It's true that you can't control what other people say or do, but you do have control over whether or not you're going to believe or accept it.

Always remember that people have reasons for the things they do. If you've ever been bullied, then you know the bully wants you to believe that it's your own fault you're being bullied. After all, if there weren't so many things wrong with you, they wouldn't be bothering you. As you know, there is a difference between someone sharing a well-intentioned and sincere piece of advice, and someone exerting their power to control a situation just because they can.

The problem is that there are people who don't have good

intentions when they say and do things to others. If you were able to dig a little deeper, you'd probably find out that most of those people are using the only tool they possess to appease their own deeply rooted lack of self-esteem. Many bullies don't even realize that the only way they can feel better about themselves is by making sure that someone else's self-esteem is lower than theirs.

Could you unmask the bully and expose them? Maybe, but I'm not suggesting you should get in a bully's face. I am suggesting that when you're away from the situation, think about the different things that might happen to someone to turn them into a bully. This also doesn't mean you should let them get away with something just because you found out (or figured out) that their life has been hard.

We all have reasons for the things we say and do. If someone is a bully, that's a choice they made, and it doesn't matter how severe their situation was or is. Being a bully is a choice. If we're the one being bullied, we have two choices. The first is how we're going to respond to what's being hurled in our direction. The second is how we're going to address how it makes us feel. It's hard not to be impacted by a bully, but none of us is obligated to take it to heart. No one can force us to believe anything we choose not to believe—not even a 600 pound gorilla. We all get to choose who we are. It starts on the inside, and when we are ready, we'll start showing it to the world.

Understanding why some people do hurtful or harmful things can't stop them from happening—especially if it's coming from someone like a parent—but it definitely can help with how *we* feel about ourselves when we don't have the power or ability to change anything else about the situation.

Always remember that you have the right to feel good

about yourself. When you aren't feeling good about yourself, take a look around and see if you can identify the source of those negative feelings. Make sure you feel good when you're with your friends and your boy/girlfriend. If you don't, what's going on that's challenging your ability to feel good about yourself? You may realize that one of your relationships has run its course. Or you may find that you don't feel like you're at your best when you're with a specific person or group. Either way, you can start figuring out ways to create some distance between you and them.

If you realize you're in one of those places where things are starting to get dark, do something different. Interrupt the negative thoughts that are trying to take over your mind by giving your brain something else to do like listening to music, dancing, running, reading, writing, cooking, gardening, drawing, etc. If all else fails, think of something nice to do for someone else. There's just something that feels really good about putting a smile on someone else's face.

Don't be so sympathetic of others that you take on their low self-esteem. People do this without realizing it. Your friend is drinking too much so you start drinking too, believing that the friend won't feel so bad or alone. Or you offer to be their designated driver, hoping that your caring will give them at least one reason to stop drinking. Sadly, that's not how it works. People are always making their own decisions about who they are. We can believe we know why someone's self-esteem is low (we might even be right) but dragging ourselves down to their level isn't going to change them. That's called enabling—making it possible for someone to continue with their behavior. It doesn't work.

By the same token, don't expect others to sacrifice their self-esteem for yours. We've all heard the saying, "Misery loves company." That may be true, but misery is no fun to hang around for very long. If that squeaky wheel is still interfering with your ability to think about anything else, you're focus is probably still on things you have no control over, like trying to figure out why someone would do or say something like that. Ask different and better questions. Figure out what you do and don't have control over. Work on the things you do have control over and your self-esteem will improve.

Pay attention. Sometimes, we don't realize our self-esteem is suffering because we're so used to what it feels like to feel bad about ourselves that it feels "wrong" when we feel good! Become aware of the difference. Don't expect to be able to monitor your self-esteem 24/7, but do check in with it once in a while so you can enjoy it when you feel good, and recognize when you need to do, think, or say something different to feel better.

What if you don't know what's wrong? What do we do when we feel really terrible about ourselves but don't know why it's happening, or what we can do to fix it? Sometimes a mood hits and we just need to experience it. It happens. Think of it as a kind of mental rain shower. Sometimes it's raining really hard; sometimes it's just a few sprinkles. Either way, it's going to run its course.

Give yourself permission to feel better. Waiting for someone or something to give us permission to feel better about ourselves doesn't work either. Even the most caring and sincere person on the planet won't be able to say or do anything helpful if we aren't open to accepting it. We may start feeling better as a result of someone or something else, but it can only take root and expand from there if we make the choice to let it.

Does Self-esteem Really Matter?

There are very successful people all over the planet who still struggle with some aspect of their self-esteem. Would it surprise you to hear that Jennifer Lopez admits to having low self-esteem? She has tremendous self-esteem when it comes to her acting, dancing, and singing skills, but suffers in relationships where she feels like so many of us do—like she's not enough.

Struggling with low self-esteem does not mean your life is going to suck. In a weird way, knowing that none of us has perfect self-esteem is a relief. We don't have to be perfect. We can make mistakes and still become the kind of person who lives a life worth dreaming about. But if we try to avoid the areas of self-esteem we struggle with, they can become the squeaky wheel threatening to take over our life.

Flexing Your Filters:

Like so many things in life, self-esteem very often reacts to triggers. Sometimes those triggers are the people around us—like when we walk past a group of people and they look at us and laugh and whisper. Even if we were feeling good, that can trigger self-doubt, and then our self-esteem levels drop.

One of the biggest triggers we have to deal with is the way we talk to ourselves. Have you ever stopped to listen to the things you say to yourself? Some of those things we say can be downright scary; as is the fact that just about everyone has looked at themselves in the mirror and called themselves a "loser."

We can't stop the running dialogue that's always going through our mind, but we can start paying attention to it and start saying good things about ourselves, to ourselves.

In this first list, write down five things that you know you say to yourself that aren't as kind or supportive as they could be. Also write down where that idea came from. Look at the list. Are these words you would feel perfectly comfortable saying to a younger brother or sister? If they aren't, then don't say them to yourself either.

1. _____

2. _____

3. _____

4. _____

5. _____

_____

In this next list, write down five things you'd like to hear on a daily basis because they'd make you feel better about yourself.

1. _____

2. _____

3. _____

4. _____

5. _____

_____

Now that you've written this list, make the choice to start replacing the words and phrases from the first list with the words and phrases on your new list.

In the future, whenever you hear an unsupportive thought going through your mind, come up with something better to think, and then kick that other thought straight out of your mind.

11

Love

There are times when love feels like the easiest thing on the planet. But then, in the blink of an eye, it can become the most complicated. There isn't a human being who has ever lived who hasn't tried to figure out what love is, what it means, if they can live without it, or if they can live with it. Some of the most enduring pieces of literature and art that exist were created with the theme of love at their core.

Love is a big thing, and it can be expressed in so many different ways! When two people deeply and truly love each other, that's one expression of love. If they have a baby together, they're likely to experience a deep and profound love for their child. That's another aspect of love. There's the love that a child will have for his or her parents, etc. There are plenty of other expressions of love too. You can love something you do and love the way something makes you feel, both of which are expressions and/or experiences of love. What about the sport you love, or the TV show that you love because it's changed your life.

We all have the same huge capacity for love. Just think about someone or something you love and how big that love feels. It feels so big that it wants to expand to anyone or anything around you, even people or things you previously hated. Maybe you always hated studying in the library, but then you fell in love with someone who does all their studying in the library. Suddenly you don't hate the idea of studying in the library as much as you used to.

We want to love, and to be loved. We all want that feeling that makes us feel like we're about to bust wide open with joy, and desperately want to avoid how it feels when some aspect of love has gone wrong. It is any wonder that love can be found at the root of so many of our issues? Clearly, our love filter has a lot of work to do, but sometimes it's easier not to think about what's going on and just give into the experience of love instead.

Why is Love Always so Complicated!

Love can be very demanding. If you've ever fallen in love, then you know what I'm talking about. Our first real experience with love—the one that makes it hard to breathe and has our stomach doing flip-flops while our heart is racing—can be very exciting. It can also take center stage. So much so that we sometimes find ourselves doing and saying things we would have never even considered doing before. Ultimately, our success (or failure) with love is going to depend on our decisions about it. Our decisions about what love means to us are going to help our love filter develop.

When we're children and our love filter is still developing, we can come up with some pretty strange ideas about how love works. Some kids grow up thinking that love happens in degrees because they believe their parents love them more when they do the right things, and less when they do the wrong things. That may sound silly, but it takes a fair amount of maturity to understand what unconditional love is. This person could grow up believing that the more they do things for the person they love, the more that person will love them.

Consider the kid who grows up with two parents who fall out of love and decide to get a divorce when he or she is eight-years-old. This kid might grow up believing that even if they fall deeply in love with someone, they're going to fall out of love with that someone too. The adult version of this could be the person who avoids commitment. Or the person who's so afraid of falling *out* of love that they do everything they can (usually unconsciously) to avoid falling *in* love.

One of the toughest choices we face in our lifetime centers around whether or not to open our heart to another person. For people who've been hurt as a child, or as an adult, even the thought of it is a risk they can't bear. Instead, they push their desires to love and be loved aside, and build walls up and around themselves to protect their hearts.

Think about people who were abused by their parents when they were children. What did their experiences teach them about love?

As children, we can only base our knowledge of what love is on the ways we experience it. If we all got the right messages about what love is—or isn't—when we were growing up, we'd all do a better job with our relationships, but we don't. We get conflicting messages. And while the "big picture" of love is great, let's face it, it's relationships that we usually struggle with. And it's the adult person-to-person relationships that we feel the most pressure to succeed with.

Take Care of Yourself First

If you've ever flown anywhere, you know the flight

attendants give a speech about what to do in the event of an emergency. One of the things they talk about is the oxygen mask. They always say, "If you have a child traveling with you, put your mask on first, and then theirs." Those words would make a good motto to live our lives by because if we don't take care of ourselves first, we limit the degree to which we can take care of anyone else. If we don't learn to love ourselves first—with all our quirks, weird habits, physical embarrassments, etc.—how can we possibly love someone else's quirks, weird habits, physical embarrassments, etc.!

As cliché as it sounds, being able to love someone else honestly and openly begins with being able to love ourselves first. And people who struggle with low self-esteem very often struggle with love too. It makes sense. When you love someone, you want them to know how great you think they are, so you tell them, or do things to show them. How would it make you feel if the person you loved didn't believe your kind words or deeds, or wouldn't accept that there might be something great about them just because you say there is? It would make you feel like you're thoughts, beliefs, and opinions didn't matter to them—and then you'd end up not feeling good about yourself either. Any way you look at it, not feeling good about yourself can be toxic to a relationship.

There are lots of sad examples of what happens in relationships between two people who don't love themselves, like when a man starts hitting the woman he "loves." The woman tries to convince herself that the only reason he hits her is because he gets frustrated or angry, and that it won't happen again. He may want to believe that too, but his dad hit his mom, and they're still together, so even though he might not like doing it, he might think hitting is just part of a relationship.

Low self-esteem and a lack of self-love and acceptance go hand-in-hand, and it isn't fair to expect other people to love us enough to fill the voids we have in ourselves. That's a one-way relationship with one person doing all the giving while the other is doing all the taking—and that quickly gets old for the person doing all the giving. We can't expect other people to fix us.

If we want to have a loving relationship with another person, then we have to start finding and creating reasons to feel good about ourselves. One thing we can do is to look at our other relationships. Just because we might struggle with intimate relationships, that doesn't automatically mean we aren't good at being a friend, or a good sister or brother, or a good son or daughter.

Don't fall into the trap of thinking that you have to find, and then fix, everything that's wrong with you. No one is perfect, and each of us has value regardless of our shortcomings. Each of us has something of value to share with others. We are all worthy of love too. Can you remember back to when you were a little kid? Back then, you were absolutely lovable. Look at any four-year-old, and you'll see that they're all perfectly lovable itty-bitty human beings. That part of us doesn't goes away just because we grow up. It's still a part of us; it was just a lot easier to access when we were younger—before life and love started getting complicated. Remembering that there's a part of you that is both worthy and capable of love is a very good place to start feeling better about yourself.

Some people get stuck in the trap of feeling like they've made so many mistakes that they're no longer worthy of being loved. They might even grow to hate themselves, and there's very little anyone else can do to convince them otherwise. This is one place where role models can help, and it's not like you have to look hard to find them. Our world is full of people who've made mistakes, sometimes huge mistakes, and then turned their lives around. They follow different turn-around paths, but those paths all start with one simple, very important realization: Human beings make mistakes! Let go of the person you were, and start loving the person you're becoming!

Loving yourself first can make a profound difference in your relationships. It's the difference between a relationship where love is shared between two hearts, and a relationship where the amount of love to be shared is limited by each individual's level of self-esteem and self-love.

The Benefits of Loving and Accepting Yourself

There are real benefits to loving yourself. Think about the ways people who don't love themselves tend to treat other people. People who don't love themselves don't want the people around them feeling good about themselves. When they're around people who are happy, or seem to be comfortable with who they are, they're more likely to do or say something to make sure those people start doubting themselves, or feel worse about themselves.

You probably know people like this. They meet someone new, and ten seconds later, they're making negative assumptions about that person. It's not uncommon for teen girls—especially those who are insecure—to ridicule another girl for being "too fat" or "ugly" because they don't feel comfortable with themselves. They pick on the other girl so they can trick themselves into feeling better about who they are. It's the same for boys who bully or torment other boys too.

Unfortunately, as part of my work, I see kids go to extremes to fill the voids they feel. Whether it's being promiscuous, or having a baby as a teen, the end result is always the same: The void remains because they don't know how to love themselves first. Some teen girls believe that if they have sex with a boy, then he is sure to value her, or love her. But love isn't the cause or result of sex. The same can be said for having a baby. Surely a baby will provide love without condition. Right? Wrong. Having a baby when you aren't prepared is a selfish act, even when it's a genuine attempt to feel real love.

The reason these scenarios rarely ever lead to real love is because they are acts chosen through a blurred and confused love filter. As teens begin to sort out what love is, and how to respect and love themselves first, they will see that they can find love without compromising themselves, and without acting selfishly.

The Choice Factor

As with so many other points in this book, once again it's important to understand the role of choice here. In many ways, the need to have someone to love, and for someone to love us, can be so strong that it feels like we don't have a choice. We always have a choice though. Always, always, always.

Don't kid yourself into believing that giving away "love" in the form of sex, or sticking around because you "love" someone when that someone is treating you badly is the result of a deep and profound love. If you love yourself, you'll see that what the other person feels for you is just a very small piece of what a really good relationship feels like. Do you remember reading about anchors and balloons? Well, real love is definitely a balloon. The *almost* love is definitely an anchor that will hold you in place right where you are until you make the decision that it's not enough, and that you'd like to have something better in your life.

People who are miserable and doing their best to make sure that the people they hang around feel worse than they do are also filled with the need to be loved and to give love. So don't buy into what you see on the surface when they go out of their way to prove that they don't care about anyone or anything. By the same token, don't feel like it's your responsibility to go out of your way to prove to them that they are lovable. You can, but that decision requires a lot of thought because some of those people will not take kindly to your good intentions.

Lastly, please understand that there is a difference between the love you might have for someone and how you feel about what that person did. For example, with time and work you might come to love an abusive parent simply because they gave you life, but that doesn't mean you have to love or accept what they did to you in any way.

The Rewards of Love's Many Aspects

Having read about love now, can you see how easy it is to misunderstand what's really going on? One of the most devastating consequences of this confusion is when someone passes their misinterpretations of love down to their children.

Anyone who has been abused by a parent—even a distant or uncaring one—will tell you that breaking that cycle is hard. We can't go inside someone else's mind to fix or change their thinking. Nor can we know what's going on in someone else's mind and heart when it comes to love. Like it is with so many of life's situations, we can only really know what's going on inside of us.

One of the most rewarding results of considering your own thoughts about love first is being able to make decisions about what feels right or wrong for you. There is so much about love to look forward to. There's nothing quite like seeing other people happy because of the love we've given them. Love can help us, heal us, encourage us, and inspire us. It can give us purpose and a reason to muster up our courage to take a leap and make changes. It can guide us through our rough patches, and endure over time and distance.

We've all heard the saying, "Better to have loved and lost than never to have loved at all." It may be true, but it only refers to one aspect of love. Granted, it's probably the most popular, but it isn't the only way to experience love. Keep your mind open, and you're sure to start recognizing life's many opportunities to experience giving and receiving love.

Flexing Your Filters:

Our love filter is very powerful, but like all the other filters we've talked about, it can be influenced by our fears. What makes love so powerful is that when we choose love, it very often cancels out fear. You've probably heard stories about people who've lifted a car off a child. That's a very physical example of love defeating fear in action.

Because fear has the ability to interfere with self-love too, let's start with that. In this first list, write down ten things you already love about yourself. They can be anything—even things like loving the color of your hair or eyes. Don't stop until you have all ten.

1. _____

2. _____

3. _____

4. _____

5. _____

6. _____

7. _____

8. _____

_____

9. _____

_____

10. _____

_____

This second list is for ten things about you that other people *should* love about you. It doesn't have to be something they've told you or said about you either. This list can include things like, "Because I'm very loyal to my friends."

1. _____

_____

2. _____

_____

3. _____

_____

4. _____

_____

5. _____

_____

6. _____

_____

7. _____

_____

8. _____

_____

9. _____

_____

10. _____

_____

The one thing you might realize at the end of these first two lists is that if the people you're hanging out with, or having relationships with, don't get that you bring some great stuff to the relationship, maybe they aren't the right people to hang around. In this last list, write down the five most important people in your life. Then write down what it is that you love about each person the most.

1. _____

2. _____

3. _____

4. _____

5. _____

One of the wonderful things about love is that as soon as you get acquainted with what genuine love looks and feels like, you're going realize how much of it there is to go around.

12

The Plan

When do you think you'll be ready to make the "big" choices in your life? Are you already making those kinds of choices? Or are you still floundering a bit? It would be understandable if you were struggling. Look at the adults around you. Plenty of them are still struggling and they're a lot older than you.

The things you've read about in this book aren't exactly common topics of discussion either. One reason is because there are adults who like it better when younger people respect and obey them. True, it's an outdated concept, but that doesn't make it any less true. There have always been, and will always be, people who feel the need to have power over others.

But you have power too, and you should never forget that. Life doesn't just happen to you. It's not some uncontrollable force waiting to consume you and spit you out at its whim. Before you read this book, a lot of your power was at the mercy of all the people who influenced your filters with their views and beliefs about life. As long as their ideas were all you knew, they could influence and determine what you saw and thought and did. They could convince you that your choices weren't yours to make. They had power over you.

Now you're at the end of this book, and you've had time to work on your filters. You've realized things about yourself, and most likely about many of the people around you. You might have even glimpsed what it feels like when you start recognizing the power you have to start taking steps towards the things that have meaning to you.

Of course it doesn't stop with reading this book. It doesn't stop with doing the exercises in it either. That would be like going for a two mile jog one day and thinking that would be enough exercise to keep you fit for the rest of your life. You still have work to do, but it's both good and rewarding work. It's the kind of work that makes you feel good about what you can do today. There is an ancient Sanskrit poem that reads:

> Look to this day
> for it is life
> the very life of life.
> In its brief course lie all
> the realities and truths of existence
> the joy of growth
> the splendor of action
> the glory of power.
> For yesterday is but a memory
> And tomorrow is only a vision.
> But today well lived
> makes every yesterday a memory of happiness
> and every tomorrow a vision of hope.
> Look well, therefore, to this day.

Some of the work ahead of you will be trial and error. It takes practice to strike the balance between figuring out which thoughts and ideas are actually yours or someone else's, and taking control of your life using your own thoughts and ideas. There's also the issue of what to do with thoughts

144

and ideas that come from other people. After all, not all the thoughts and ideas of others are bad—not by any stretch.

Sometimes the decision is a no-brainer. If you encounter a thought, idea, or belief about yourself that makes you think less of yourself or of what you can do, what you want to do, or what is possible for you, kick it to the curb. Replace it with the truth that you have something valuable to contribute— because we all do. And I'm not just talking about big things and big dreams like being the President. For most of us, the contributions we make will be more specific and take place within the circle of our immediate lives. It won't matter how many people know about it either because many of those actions fill us up beyond anything we could have imagined.

Understanding your filters doesn't mean the thoughts, beliefs, and ideas you've started claiming as your own won't be challenged. They will. It can be stressful when this happens, but it also feels really good when you work through those challenges.

People are going to challenge your filters too. But you've been experiencing that since you've been old enough to recognize when you didn't like the way something was going. The first few times it happens to you from now on, you're likely to fall right back into the ways you used to respond. Just recognize when it's happening, and remind yourself of all the good stuff you've been working on. And remember, it's not your job to fix other people's filters.

As you start to get used to dealing with challenges, there might be times when you'll feel like you want to "come out swinging" just out of sheer frustration. Probably not the best solution. But it's definitely evidence that your self-esteem is on the rise and you feel strongly about finding your own way and making your own choices. That might be hard for other people to accept because it limits the amount of power and influence they have over you and your choices. You just have to choose your battles wisely. Before a situation gets out of hand, decide if the outcome of winning the verbal or physical challenge in front of you is worth the price you're going to have to pay for it after the fact.

Darren's Plan

It may be odd to think about sitting down and starting to design a plan for your life. After all, if your filters are clean and clear of clutter, and you're feeling better about who you are, then shouldn't your life just start working out on its own? If you have a plan, doesn't that mean there won't be any room for excitement and spontaneity? Plus, how can anyone really know what their lives will be like in one, two, or ten years from now? Those are all good questions, but let's look at a plan in action.

Darren was never good at sports and always gets flustered trying to talk to girls. Most of his friends are into video games. He likes games too, but his real passion is for designing and programming apps. After doing some internet research, he found out that people who do that kind of work are called Applications Architects.

So far, he's designed three apps. His friends think they're cool, but that's as far as it's gone. It would be great if someone "found" him and hired him right out of high school, but he knows that's not likely, and he doesn't want to sit around and wait for it to happen. Instead, he's decided to go to college so he can get a degree as an "applications architect."

His parents on the other hand, have it in their minds that

he should become an attorney. They're always telling him how great of an attorney he'll be, and they talk about it like it's already a done deal. They remind him how good he's always been at debating the pros and cons of the rules they've set for him, and talk about his gift for talking himself out of sticky situations. There are already several attorneys in the family too, so he's just about guaranteed a profitable and stable career if he does what they want him to do.

When Darren talks to his parents, he's able to talk about his dream of becoming an applications architect without hesitation. But when he's on his own, he worries. What if his parents are right? What if he can't make a living designing and programming apps? Should he even take the risk?

And then he stops and reminds himself that he's thought this out. He understands his parent's perspective, but in truth, he could fail at either career so why shouldn't he try for the one that he feels good about. He's done his research about the job too. He's looked at the curriculum he'll have to follow and even though he knows that some of it will be tough, he believes he can do it. He knows he'll have to prove himself to land a good job too, but he knows that if he does well in school, he'll be one step closer to landing the job he wants.

It would be easy to look at Darren and decide that he's brave, or maybe a natural risk taker, but he isn't either of those things. Darren's a regular guy who just did what this book set him up to do. Instead of accepting the ideas, thoughts, and information other people were using to try and influence his decision, he took the time he needed to make his own decision based on what he thinks and believes is best for him in the long run.

Another thing he did was to break down the next few years so he could think about what was ahead of him, looking for any potential obstacles he'd have to deal with. For example, he was definitely worried about the math classes because math was his worst subject. But after doing more research he found out that the college he wanted to go to had a great tutoring program.

Will Darren succeed? There's no way for any of us to answer that question. Even Darren can't answer that question, whether he decides to become an applications architect or an attorney. But, by coming up with a plan, he's certainly setting himself up to succeed. In the end, he'll succeed or fail according to his own effort. If he's determined to pass all his classes with excellent grades, it's within his power to turn that goal into a reality. If he succeeds, the glory of accomplishment is all his. If he fails, well, that responsibility is all his too.

We can learn from Darren because we're all in his situation to some degree. There will always be people in our lives who think they know better than we do. Some of them will be well-intentioned, some of them won't.

In many ways, coming up with a plan is a way of proving to ourselves that we can do something. A plan gives us something within our power to work on. Having a plan takes out some of the anxiety and stress we'd be feeling without it. Plans give us the opportunity to objectively consider the obstacles that might get in our way.

Darren's plan may not sound glamorous, but it doesn't have to. He likes his plan because of the result it leads to. Life may throw in a few unexpected turns—it always does. He might have to get a job to help pay for college, but one of his teachers might have connections at a company Darren would love to work for. Something could happen that forces him to take a semester or year off, but he might meet an amazing girl.

No one can know exactly what's going to happen in their

future, but a plan allows us to be proactive about what we do. Without a plan, we're at the mercy of everyone else's choices and decisions. And this applies just as much to plans that everyone in our lives—including us—agree with. If Darren couldn't wait to be an attorney, he would still benefit from actively makings plans.

Your Feelings Matter Too

When people think about planning their future, they forget they can also decide **who** they want to be. It's true that our thoughts, feelings, attitudes, and views of the world may change over time, but that's not a reason to wait to make decisions about the kind of person we want to be today.

We can add other things to our plan too. We can think about the kind of people we want to have as friends and co-workers, and about the person we want to spend our life with. There are some books that will tell you to write down every detail about those people so you'll know them when you see them. But don't get too hung up on actual physical descriptions. When you think about the people you want in your life, you're experiencing what it might feel like to be in the presence of those people, and what it might be like to spend time with them. Yes, you might think you prefer blonde hair over brown, but better questions are: What is it about the blonde hair that makes you feel a certain way? Do you think of people with blonde hair as more laid back or more fun? Or maybe that people with brown hair tend to be boring? The answers to simple questions like that will help you understand what it is about other people that truly captures your attention.

The same goes for thinking about the kind of person you want people to think you are. Most people won't ever get to really know you because it's hard to know who someone is just by their actions. They can't see below the surface anymore than we can. You might think that making a big donation will make you look better in other people's eyes, but it's not the size or type of donation that matters. It's the fact that helping is a part of your plan. So when you add *generous* to your personal list of traits and qualities, remember that you can be generous right now. You don't have to wait until you can be hugely generous in front of an applauding audience. Why wait to feel good about you are?

A Future to Look Forward to

It's amazing how many people journey through life without any kind of plan. But if no one's explained what having a plan means, or about how important it is, how would someone even know they had a choice? If someone's never worked on their filters, they probably won't even know there's another way!

And yet there are still people who know they could change the way things are, but don't. Why? Because it's hard. For some people, it feels like such an impossible leap that they end up stuck in their role as victim for their entire life. I don't want you to fall into that trap.

Our actions are like rocks thrown in a pond, each ripple impacting the people around us. If the idea of creating a plan is still a struggle, think about these questions. Are you planning on having children? What do want their life to be like? Do you want them to have good self-esteem? Do you want them to grow up feeling confident? Again, there are no guarantees, but the first example your children will have in their lives will come from you. What do you want to teach them? If drugs and alcohol are a part of your current plan, will it be okay with you if it becomes part of their plan too?

We do better in life when we formulate plans. Many of life's big goals take advanced planning. Creating a plan during your waking hours will make it easier to sleep at night too. We start losing sleep when we start losing our sense of control and power over what's going on in our lives.

Plans work even better when they are revisited, updated, and revised on a regular basis. The best part about revisiting a plan is that you get to see how much you've already accomplished. How often you want to go over a plan is up to you, and it's different for everyone. People who are control freaks might feel like they have to have every minute of every day mapped out. If you know someone like that, you also know how crazy that kind of micro-managing can get.

How often should you think about your plans? Once a year? Twice a year? It's your choice, and sometimes it depends on what's going on in your life at that moment. For example, it's okay to think about who you'd like to work for after you graduate from college four years from now, but too soon to pencil in your interviews. You might change your mind about who you'd like to work for after school. Or discover something you're even more excited about pursuing and change your major.

Facing the Unknown

As you head off into the "real" world, whether that's life

after college, or life after high school, you'll likely have more questions than answers. That kind of uncertainty can be frightening at any age, but as a teenager it carries a special weight. The decisions that teenagers make are some of the biggest of any age group. Do I go to college? If I do, what major do I pick? If I don't, what should I do for a living? But there are other decisions you will be making too, like how having sex or experimenting with drugs might affect you in the long run.

Having a plan allows you to work within a framework, and that gives you peace of mind. Even if you're a spontaneous person, a plan will give you the security of knowing that by operating within a framework, you'll still be moving in a direction of your own choosing—even if you do end up taking an occasional side trip.

Darren's hypothetical situation was a good example of what facing the unknown can look like, and that when you have a plan, even if it's general and loose, it's like having a GPS in a world without street signs. It helps you find your way, even if you do decide to change your destination.

Here are just two more quick things to share with you:

1. ***Give yourself permission to make mistakes.*** We all make them—big ones and small ones—and very often it's not the mistake we'll remember as much as the lesson that comes along with it. The only real mistake is not taking advantage of what you've learned from the lesson.

2. ***Don't overwhelm yourself with feeling like you have to figure everything out right this minute.*** Give yourself time to absorb what you've read here. Give yourself time to grow and mature into the person you want to be. Use

what you've learned about yourself to come up with plans that keep you moving you in directions that make you feel good about yourself, good about what you're accomplishing, and good about the impact you're having on the people and the world around you. That's the kind of groundwork that leads to a purposeful and meaningful life.

The Last Exercise

It's easy to read a book and get all excited by everything you've learned, but it's easy to forget what you've read too. This last exercise is an opportunity to list the ideas and thoughts you'd really like to remember. So, for each chapter listed, write down what was most interesting, memorable, and/or meaningful to you about that specific chapter. Then, whenever you pick up the book, you can flip right to this page and be reminded. It's like you're creating your own index.

Chapter 2: Whose Life is it? (Aka The Blame Chapter)

_____
_____
_____
_____
_____

Chapter 3: Competition

_____
_____
_____
_____
_____

Chapter 4: A Sense of Self

_____
_____
_____
_____
_____

Chapter 5: Role Models

_____

_____

_____

_____

_____

_____

Chapter 6: Fear versus F.E.A.R.

_____

_____

_____

_____

_____

Chapter 7: How Fear Impacts Our Choices

_____

_____

_____

_____

_____

Chapter 8: Choices

_____

_____

_____

_____

_____

Chapter 9: Experiences

_____

_____

_____

_____

_____

Chapter 10: Self-Esteem – How do You Like Me Now?

_____

_____

_____

_____

_____

Chapter 11: Love

_____

_____

_____

_____

_____

Chapter 12: The Plan

_____

_____

_____

_____

_____

This is one of the longest exercises in this book too, but it's also one of the most important. As each of us continues to grow and mature—regardless of how old we are—we discover that lessons have layers. You learn something, and then when you apply what you've learned, you discover something else about it.

That's the way it is with the ideas we covered in this book, and that's the way it is with our filters. They are always growing with us. The more choices and decisions we make about who we are, the more unique and complex our filters become. They become strong too, because we've taken the time to think about them.

I've said this plenty of times in this book, but it's so important, it's worth saying one last time. Even the act of deciding to not make a choice is a choice. Everything begins with that first choice, the one you make in favor of yourself, the one where you give yourself permission to choose who you are, and who you want to be. You can do this. And reaching the end of this book is absolute evidence that you're capable of making choices that can change your life for the better. Your choices won't always be perfect, but at least they'll be yours.

About the Author

Jeff Londraville is a speaker, actor, author, coach and 20-year seasoned educator. His knowledge of personal development is rooted in his Bachelor of Arts Degree in Sociology and Masters Degree in Education with coursework in Psychology, as well as extensive experience as an educator and mentor to youth. He is also a former Team USA hockey player and long-time hockey coach.

Jeff has been featured as a personal development expert on various television and radio programs throughout the Northeast, and shares his book and message with people of all ages via national and international speaking engagements.

Jeff currently resides with his wife and two daughters in Longmeadow, Massachusetts.

If you'd like to schedule Jeff for a speaking engagement, send an email to Londraville8@gmail.com, or find him on Facebook – Jeff Londraville.